SOUTH YORKSHIRE
RAILWAY STATIONS

Mexborough railway station staff; the woman in the centre is possibly Annie Grant.

The first train on the Penistone to Sheffield via Barnsley rail link, 16 May 1983. (Reproduced courtesy of *Sheffield Newspapers*)

SOUTH YORKSHIRE
RAILWAY STATIONS
Adwick-le-Street to Wortley

PETER TUFFREY

AMBERLEY

Above is Elscar railway station, with Woodhouse railway station featured below.

First published 2011

Amberley Publishing
The Hill, Stroud
Gloucestershire GL5 4ER

www.amberleybooks.com

British Library Cataloguing in Publication Data.
A catalogue record for this book is available from the British Library.

ISBN 978-1-4456-0122-9

Typesetting and Origination by Amberley Publishing.
Printed in Great Britain.

Contents

Acknowledgements

I would like to thank the following people for their help: Roy Andrews, Jim Firth, Stephen Gay, Stuart Hastings, John Law, Paul License, Hugh Parkin, Derek Porter, Jane Salt, Douglas Thompson, Tristram Tuffrey and Geoff Warnes.

Special thanks is due to everyone at *Wikipedia*. Further gratitude may be expressed to John Law and Stephen Gay for looking though the final proofs.

First electric train to leave Sheffield Victoria railway station, 14 September 1954. (Reproduced courtesy of *Sheffield Newspapers*)

Introduction

I've always wanted to live in a railway station – an abandoned one, but with the tracks still intact so that I could leisurely watch the trains go by in the comfort of my own unique home. I would not be bothered whether I saw steam or diesel locomotives; I have an interest in both. That fantasy is linked to my first interest in railways, which came about through my maternal grandparents living in a house at Denaby Main, adjacent to the Great Central line between Sheffield and Doncaster. As a small boy I stood transfixed on their front room window ledge watching the last days of steam trail by and new gleaming diesel-electric locos make their first appearance.

My thoughts of living in a railway station were further enhanced in the late 1970s when I met renowned pop artist Peter Blake, who himself lived and set up a studio in Wellow station. The way in which he had made it homely fascinated me, albeit without any tracks outside and trains passing by.

But enough fantasy and frivolity – why do railway stations hold such fascination for everyone interested in railways? Let's look for some answers in the stations which were once found in numbers across South Yorkshire.

Naturally, the emergence of railway stations in abundance came about with the birth of the railway industry itself, as well as the growth of the region as a thriving industrial area. So it was only a natural progression that the communities who grew up alongside it needed transport, and stations were quickly provided to facilitate travel.

That being said, railway station architecture never fails to impress or amaze. Many stations date from the nineteenth century and reflect the grandiose architecture of the time, lending prestige to the city or town as well as to railway operations and operators.

Looking at pictures of stations that have vanished as well as buildings which still exist, the sheer size and fine detail they incorporate is breathtaking. Some were almost identical in design, such as the double pavilion-style stations found in numbers along the Great Central lines. Sometimes it is difficult to tell one from another.

However, while it's hard not to be impressed with the design of old stations, it's hard to accept that their statement in architectural terms justified their building. I argue this because some of those in South Yorkshire only existed for a relatively short period. Quite a number were wrongly placed, sometimes between two villages like Tickhill and Wadworth, or were quite a distance from the community they were intended to serve. Many stations were quickly made redundant by the advent of trams, motorbuses and motor vehicles. Some were even built too late to have any use on the railway system they intended to serve, particularly those along the Hull & Barnsley route, such as York Road Doncaster and Warmsworth Doncaster, which never saw any passengers.

Of course the halts like the ones at Harlington and Edlington were at the other end of the architectural spectrum, being no more than disused railway carriages put down in a convenient spot. But were these halts a foretaste of what was to be introduced in later years? The stations currently at Goldthorpe, Chapeltown, Hatfield and Stainforth, and Thorne South may support this observation.

Another fascinating aspect of railway stations is the sheer numbers of staff they employed. One of the pictures at Chapeltown station illustrates this point admirably. Many of the staff are seen proudly posing in their uniforms alongside the stationmaster, everyone looking smart and efficient, and equally helpful and amenable. For supportive evidence of the latter please look at the picture of the porter at Millhouses railway station, he is clearly enjoying being of assistance, helping someone loading their luggage on to the waiting train.

Studying the function of old railway stations, we clearly see that they not only provided passenger and goods services, but facilities for loading and unloading livestock as well. Note the picture of the cattle dock which once stood alongside Doncaster station – amazing – and it is an activity and service that could never be found today.

Yet taking into account the architectural splendour, the volume of staff and the stations' relatively short lifespan, with some never even seeing a passenger, isn't there an element of the surreal about the entire scene? It would certainly seem that way and maybe that's what Dr Beeching saw in the 1950s and 1960s, providing him with an excuse to wield a large axe and close so many stations.

In gathering together and choosing the pictures for inclusion in this book, I attempted to find a picture of each station mentioned in the A–Z, half knowing at the outset this would be a futile task as a number of stations only lasted a few years. Some even preceded the wide use of cameras and did not even attract an artist's eye to record them. Naturally some stations were pictured more than others and provide a variety of scenes to be included here. I am particularly fond of the scene on Sheffield Victoria railway station featuring the evacuees, the inspectors at Tickhill and the children waiting at Askern.

Railway stations were particularly fascinating for the armies of commercial postcard photographers who were in abundance during the first half of the twentieth century. Consequently, I have used their images in large numbers throughout this book, being grateful for their services. In my lifetime, I have been able to photograph two railway stations that have disappeared, Tickhill and Sheffield Victoria, as well as recording the reduction in buildings at Conisbrough.

Following closure, large numbers of railway stations disappeared with not a brick now remaining. Others were fortunate enough to be sensitively converted into private houses like the ones at Deepcar and Finningley. Some are greatly reduced in size, Conisbrough being an example, while others are intact but lost in overgrowth such as Sprotbrough. After closure and clearance, some have reopened while others have been stripped of all buildings yet still operate services; Bolton-on-Dearne and Hatfield and Stainforth being examples.

Instead of merely producing a picture/caption book I wanted to list every known railway station that existed in South Yorkshire as well as including as many pictures as possible. Because of the enormity of the task and space available, the information included is kept to a bare minimum. Maybe some more stations will come to light after publication, as new information has a habit of appearing once a book is published. But that it is OK, it can be included when somebody else decides to tackle the subject.

Hopefully this book will keep alive and add to everyone's fascination about South Yorkshire railway stations. It will certainly underpin my interest. Unfortunately, it looks rather doubtful whether I will ever live in a railway station. Nevertheless, I will persevere with the National Lottery as I have a keen eye on the disused station at Adwick and Carcroft with the main line between Leeds and Doncaster still passing by. Wish me luck!

CHAPTER ONE

Adwick-le-Street and Carcroft Railway Station to Broughton Lane Railway Station

Adwick-le-Street and Carcroft railway station, looking north.

Entrance leading to Adwick-le-Street and Carcroft railway station.

Adwick-le-Street and Carcroft railway station, facing north.

Adwick Station

Adwick railway station opened in March 1866 as an intermediate stop on the West Riding and Grimsby Railway's main line from Wakefield Westgate to Doncaster. According to *Wikipedia*: 'After first being called 'Adwick' it was renamed Adwick-le-Street and Carcroft in 1867'. The station's main building – still standing today, though no longer part of the present station – comprised of a booking office, a waiting room, and a station master's house. Situated on the Doncaster-bound (up) platform, it was constructed of rock-faced stone, with hipped roofs and a spire which was part of the living quarters. The Leeds-bound (Down) platform was

The abandoned Adwick-le-Street and Carcroft railway station, photograph taken on 3 January 2011.

served by a small wooden, enclosed waiting shelter. On 1 May 1880 the name was changed to 'Carcroft and Adwick-le-Street'. This station was closed for goods traffic in June 1965 and for passengers on 6 November 1967. Adwick was reopened by the South Yorkshire Passenger Transport Executive, with new platforms to the south-east of the original station site, on 11 October 1993. The new station possesses a footbridge and a road bridge allowing traffic and pedestrians to pass unhindered from parking to platform 2.

The new Adwick railway station, photograph taken on 3 January 2011.

Anston railway station

Anston railway station was situated on the Great Central and Midland Railway Joint line between North Anston and South Anston near Rotherham. Passenger services on the line (under the control of the South Yorkshire Joint Committee) began on 7 December 1910 and were jointly operated by the Great Central Railway and the Great Northern Railway. The station (built after the opening of the line) opened to traffic on 20 May 1912. It was a double platform station with waiting shelters on each side. The station closed in 1929, but the line's freight services passed to the Eastern Region of British Railways on nationalisation in 1948. Since closure to passengers the line has been visited regularly by Enthusiasts Specials travelling over all or part of the line.

Anston railway station.

Arksey railway station

Arksey railway station, serving the villages of Arksey and Stockbridge, was on the main line between Doncaster and York. It was opened by the Great Northern Railway on 6 June 1848 as Stockbridge; during December 1850 it was renamed Arksey and Stockbridge and in September 1854 it was renamed Arksey. The station became part of the London and North Eastern Railway during the Grouping of 1923, passing on to the Eastern Region of British Railways during the nationalisation of 1948. It was then closed by British Railways on 5 August 1952.

Arksey railway station looking south.

Arksey railway station facing north, 30 July 1952.

Attercliffe Road railway station

Attercliffe Road railway station, near Attercliffe Road in Attercliffe, Sheffield, served the communities of Attercliffe, Burngreave and the workers in the Don Valley. It was opened by the Midland Railway in 1870 at the same time as the main line from Chesterfield. Having two platforms, the station was positioned above Effingham Street, although access was from a gated path from Leveson Street; an underpass led to an inclining bridge on to the Down platforms. The station became part of the London Midland and Scottish Railway during the Grouping of 1923, passing on to the London Midland Region of British Railways upon nationalisation in 1948. When sectorisation was introduced in the 1980s, the station was served by Regional Railways in co-operation with the South Yorkshire PTE until the privatisation of British Rail. By the 1980s, only certain morning and evening peak trains called at the station, as stopping trains exacerbated capacity problems in the major bottleneck north of Sheffield Midland. By the early 1990s the dearth of industry in the area had caused the station's patronage to dwindle to a level where closure was easily justified, again with line capacity constraints being quoted as the reason, with the end coming in 1995.

Attercliffe railway station. (*Douglas Thompson*)

Attercliffe railway station

Attercliffe railway station was built to serve the Parish of Attercliffe cum Darnall, then separated from (but now part of) the City of Sheffield. Opened in August 1871, it was situated on the Manchester, Sheffield and Lincolnshire Railway company's line between Woodburn Junction and Tinsley Junction, which was served by trains between Sheffield Victoria, Barnsley and Rotherham Central. The station consisted of two platforms flanking the lines and these were linked by a subway. The station closed on 31 December 1900 and was replaced by a new structure which opened the following day. Joining the Great Central Railway, it became part of the London and North Eastern Railway during the Grouping of 1923, only to close on 26 September 1927.

Askern railway station

Askern railway station was on the former Lancashire & Yorkshire Railway Line between Doncaster and Knottingley. It served the village of Askern and opened on 6 June 1848, becoming part of the London Midland and Scottish Railway during the Grouping of 1923. It closed to passenger traffic in March 1947, but remained open for goods traffic for a further seventeen years. The station passed to the Eastern Region of British Railways on nationalisation. Recent proposals and developments are mentioned on Wikipedia:

Askern railway station.

The entrance to Askern railway station.

Trains still pass the site (as the line is still open for freight traffic and the occasional diverted passenger train), although there is no station at Askern today. From May 2010 regular passenger trains (operated by Grand Union) will return to the line but not to Askern as no station is immediately planned. In September 2008, as part of Doncaster Borough Councils report on rail corridors in the borough Askern, along with 7 other sites, it was listed as one of the stations suitable for reopening in the future.

Askern railway station, 27 August 1974. (Reproduced courtesy of *Sheffield Newspapers*)

Barnby Dun railway station looking east.

Barnby Dun railway station

Barnby Dun railway station was on the South Yorkshire Railway's line between Doncaster and Thorne serving Barnby Dun, near Doncaster. The original line followed the canal bank closely and the station was resited when the line was 'straightened' in the 1860s. The original station, which was situated across the canal from the village, was opened with the line on 7 July 1856 and closed on 1 October 1866, when the new station, at the opposite side of the village, was opened. The rebuilt station consisted of flanking platforms with its main buildings, in yellow engineers brick, on the Thorne-bound (up) platform. The station was again rebuilt to accommodate four tracks in the Doncaster to Thorne widening of 1913, when the Doncaster-bound (Down) platform was moved back. The station closed on 4 September 1967. The station building was demolished in July 2008.

Barnby Dun railway station facing west.

Barnby Dun railway station facing west, photograph taken on 3 January 2011.

Barnsley Court House railway station, photograph taken on 12 March 1959. (Reproduced courtesy of *Sheffield Newspapers*)

Barnsley Court House railway station

Before Barnsley Court House railway station was built, the Midland Railway's Barnsley station was at Cudworth on the former North Midland Railway's line between Leeds and Derby. To reach the town, in the 1860s, the Midland opened a line from Cudworth South Junction to Barnsley and a new, albeit temporary, station (Regent Street railway station) in Barnsley. The M.R. opened the line for goods traffic in April 1869 and for passengers on 1 May the following year.

The Midland Railway built a new passenger station on the Regent Street site and this opened for business on 23 August 1873. On 20 January 1872 the Midland Railway completed the purchase of the Old Court House, which fronted onto Regent Street, to incorporate the building into their new construction as a ticket office and waiting room; the new station was named 'Court House'. The station had an overall glass roof over its two through platforms and there was also a short 'bay' platform (No. 3) at the Penistone end of the station.

The station was controlled by two signal boxes, Court House, a small box which sat on the south end of platform 2, and Barnsley Goods Yard, which also controlled the bay platform (No .3), the cattle dock and the goods yard.

The station closed on 19 April 1960, and all rail services transferred to the Exchange Station. The Regent Street site was used as a temporary home for Barnsley's famous Open-Air markets until a new market complex was completed. The Old Court House was preserved and is now a pub/restaurant, but the rest of the structure was demolished in the early 1970s.

Barnsley Interchange (formerly Barnsley Exchange Station)

Barnsley Interchange (formerly Barnsley Exchange Station) railway station was opened as Barnsley on 1 January 1850. The original operating company was the Sheffield, Rotherham, Barnsley, Wakefield, Huddersfield & Goole Railway; pre-grouping the Lancashire and Yorkshire Railway and post-grouping the London, Midland and Scottish Railway. On 2 June 1924 the station was renamed Barnsley Low Town; 1 August 1924, 13 June 1960, Barnsley and 20 May 2007, Barnsley Interchange.Barnsley Exchange was built with only one platform. An additional platform was built to facilitate the closure of Court House.

Barnsley railway station, photograph taken on 20 June 1973. (Reproduced courtesy of *Sheffield Newspapers*)

Barnsley railway railway station. (Reproduced courtesy of *Sheffield Newspapers*)

Bawtry railway station

Bawtry railway station on the Great Northern Railway main line between Retford and Doncaster opened on 4 September 1849. The main buildings were on the town (Down) side of the line. The station was unique in its structures, these being highly individual. The main building had a small portico leading to the booking office at the front with all the usual facilities within the building. Platform shelters were in wood in the typical style of the GNR. Bawtry station was used by Royalty attending Doncaster races, but closed to passengers on 6 October 1958 and on 30 April 1971 goods facilities were withdrawn. The buildings and long platforms have been swept away, but a couple of goods yard buildings are now houses. In a report to Doncaster Borough Council in September 2008 land near the station has been protected should the site be required as a new station, with car parking facilities, in the future as the town grows.

Bawtry railway station looking north.

Bawtry railway station looking north.

The entrance to Bawtry railway station.

Bawtry railway station in a dilapidated condition.

Beauchief and Abbeydale railway station, *c. 1900*.

Beauchief railway station

Beauchief railway station (pronounced Beechif) was in Sheffield, serving the communities of Beauchief, Woodseats and Ecclesall and was situated on the Midland Main Line between Millhouses railway station and Dore & Totley station, near Abbeydale Road South in Beauchief. Opening on 1 February 1870 with two platforms, the station was originally called Abbey Houses; Beauchief 1 April 1870; Beauchief and Abbey Dale 1 May 1874; 1901 –3 expanded to four platforms; 19 March 1914 renamed Beauchief. The station was opened on the site of Hutcliffe Mill at the same time as the main line from Chesterfield. It closed on 1 January 1961, and the site is now occupied by a nursing home, although the nearby Abbeydale Station Hotel survives as the Beauchief Hotel.

Beauchief and Abbeydale railway station, photograph taken in 1961.

Beighton railway station.

Beighton railway station

Beighton railway station lies where the line of the Sheffield and Lincolnshire Junction Railway (S&LJR) crosses Rotherham Road. The first station was on the North Midland Railway (NMR), but was closed in 1843 and may have been little more than a halt.

The first section of line built by the S&LJR was between Sheffield and a junction with the NMR just south of Beighton. This was to enable a revenue-earning service to Eckington to commence and give connections to North Midland trains.

A new station was provided at the junction and some way from the centre of population. At the first push to the south by the Manchester, Sheffield and Lincolnshire Railway (The Derbyshire Lines), the final station was rebuilt by the level crossing on Rotherham Road. It was opened on 1 November 1893 with two platforms and closed exactly sixty-one years later. Pre-grouping operations were by the Sheffield and Lincolnshire Junction Railway; post-grouping London and North Eastern Railway and London Midland Region of British Railways

Beighton railway station during floods 3 February 1950.

Bentley railway station. (*Hugh Parkin*)

Bentley railway station

Bentley railway station serves Bentley, near Doncaster. It lies on the Wakefield Line and is managed by Northern Rail, who also provide all the passenger trains serving it. Bentley is a popular commuting station for Leeds and Wakefield and has a large car park for the size of the station.

Bentley Crossing Halt

Bentley Crossing Halt was a halt on the line between Doncaster and Carcroft and Adwick-le-Street.

Bessacarr railway Halt

Bessacarr railway Halt was on the Great Northern and Great Eastern Joint Railway in the suburbs of Doncaster. It opened in 1912, but did not appear in public timetables and was closed in 1924. The site of Bessacarr halt, along with seven others, was highlighted as a possible 'new station' under a report to Doncaster Borough Council in September 2008, with reopening at some future date a possibility (*The Star*, Saturday 14 February 2009).

Birdwell & Hoyland Common railway station

Bridewell and Hoyland railway station was on the South Yorkshire Railway's Blackburn Valley line between Westwood and High Royds. Intending to serve the villages of Pilley, Birdwell and Hoyland Common, near Barnsley, the original chosen site was moved half a mile nearer towards Barnsley for the use of the Earl of Wharncliffe who was, at that time, sinking Wharncliffe Silkstone Colliery nearby. This move made the station less convenient for most of the population. Opening in February 1855, the station building had an ornate canopy over its entrance and the buildings contained a private waiting room for the Earl of Wharncliffe's use. Post-grouping the station came under the London and North Eastern Railway and was closed on 7 December 1953.

Birdwell and Hoyland railway station.

Birdwell and Hoyland railway station.

Bolton-on-Dearne railway station

Bolton-on-Dearne railway station was opened by the Swinton and Knottingley Railway on 1 July 1879, and was originally named Hickleton. On 1 November 1879 it was renamed Bolton-on-Dearne, altered again on 15 January 1924 to 'Bolton-on-Dearne For Goldthorpe', before reverting back to 'Bolton-on-Dearne' on 12 June 1961.

Work to renew platforms (increasing height and resurfacing), provide new waiting shelters and lighting was completed in November 2007. A new footbridge was opened in April 2010.

Bolton-on-Dearne railway station.

Bramwith railway station

Built by the West Riding and Grimsby Railway, Bramwith was named Barnby Dun on opening, *c.* 1872, due to its close proximity to the village of that name. It took the name Bramwith (from around 1889) from the village of Kirk Bramwith, near Doncaster, although it was over two miles away. This was possibly to avoid confusion with the Barnby Dun station rebuilt on the Manchester, Sheffield and Lincolnshire Railway's straightened line between Doncaster and Thorne. The station was also closer to the village of Thorpe-in-Balne, to the north, than Kirk Bramwith itself. The station never boasted a regular-stopping passenger service, being used by excursion passenger trains travelling between the West Riding Woollen District towns and Cleethorpes from opening, until the early years of the twentieth century, after which it continued as a goods station, traffic being mostly for the agricultural market.

Brightside railway station

Brightside railway station in Sheffield served Brightside and Wincobank and was situated on the Midland Main Line on Holywell Road, lying between Attercliffe Road and Holmes railway station. Opening in 1838, at the same time as the Sheffield and Rotherham Railway from Wicker station, Brightside had two platforms, although four tracks went through. The two outside tracks were for freight use while the two inside tracks were used by both stopping and express trains.

Brightside railway station, view looking north-east, 23 April 1961. (*Ben Brooksbank*)

Brightside railway station.

Despite the opening of Meadowhall Interchange in 1990, the station remained open until 1995. A limited service had continued in its last three years and the standard South Yorkshire style bus shelter that had replaced the station buildings by the early 1980s was removed in early 2006. A footbridge spans across the three remaining tracks and both sets of stairs to the platforms are boarded.

Bridgehouses railway station

Bridgehouses railway station was the terminal station of the Sheffield, Ashton-under-Lyne and Manchester Railway from its opening in 1845 until the opening of the Wicker Arches, a 660-yard (600 metre) long viaduct across the Don Valley, which supported the new Sheffield Victoria opened on 15 September 1851. By this time the railway operating company had become the Manchester, Sheffield and Lincolnshire Railway, which in 1899 became the Great Central Railway. From 1851, Bridgehouse became the company's terminal for goods and cattle traffic. It remained open for freight until 1965. Part of the station site is now used as a car park and part of the retaining wall along Nursery Street has been demolished to make way for the northern section of Sheffield's Inner Ring Road.

Broughton Lane railway station.

Broughton Lane

Serving the communities of Darnall, Attercliffe and Carbrook, Broughton Lane railway station in Sheffield opened on 1 August 1864. This was along with the South Yorkshire Railway's extension south from Tinsley Junction to Woodburn Junction, where it met the Manchester, Sheffield and Lincolnshire Railway (MS&LR). The day the line was opened the SYR became part of the MS&LR. This link allowed the MS&LR access to Barnsley and Rotherham from Sheffield Victoria. Surrounded by sidings, the station, with its main access by steps from Broughton Lane bridge, possessed two flanking platforms. Pre-grouping it was operated by the Manchester, Sheffield and Lincolnshire Railway, Great Central Railway and post-grouping London and North Eastern Railway and BR's Eastern Region. The station closed in 1956 and no trace of it remains.

CHAPTER TWO

Catcliffe Railway Station to Elsecar Railway Station

Catcliffe railway station.

Catcliffe railway station

Near Rotherham, Catcliffe was on the Sheffield District Railway, just over 1 mile (1.6 km) north of its junction with the North Midland Railway line at Treeton Junction. The line was carried on a nine-arch brick-built viaduct over the Rother Valley and the station was constructed at the northern end of this, near to the village. Catcliffe station was noted for its bleak and isolated location and locals nicknamed it 'Klondyke'. The station was opened on 30 April 1900 and had two platforms. After grouping in 1923, it was operated by the Great Central Railway, closing on 11 September 1939, re-opening on 6 October 1946 and finally closing on 17 March 1947.

Catcliffe railway station.

Chapeltown Great Central railway station.

Chapeltown Central railway station

Chapeltown Central railway station consisted of two staggered platforms linked by a footbridge and was rebuilt in the MS&LR's double pavilion style in the 1880s. It was situated on the former South Yorkshire Railway's Blackburn Valley line between Ecclesfield East and Westwood, was also known as Chapeltown and Thorncliffe and was intended to serve Chapeltown – although it was about 1 mile (1.6 km) from its centre. It also served the works of Newton, Chambers & Company, one of the largest industrial companies in the area. The station closed to passengers on 7 December 1953 and to all traffic in April 1954.

Chapeltown railway station and staff.

Chapeltown Midland railway station.

Chapeltown railway station

Chapeltown railway station, originally known as Chapeltown South, was the first to be opened under the governance of the South Yorkshire Passenger Transport Executive on 2 August 1982; the original station, a quarter-mile (or 600 metres) nearer to Barnsley, closed at that time.

Chapeltown railway station, photograph taken on 29 July 1982.

Chapeltown railway station, photograph taken on 29 July 1982.

City Goods railway station

The London and North Western Railway opened a small goods station on Bernard Road, Sheffield in 1895. But the company subsequently obtained powers to build a more suitable establishment at the corner of Broad Street and Wharf Street, behind the Corn Exchange, three quaters of a mile west of their terminus on Bernard Road. The depot building itself was three storeys high, covered 94,260 ft^2 and possessed two 20-ton hydraulic lifts capable of carrying 10-ton wagons down to the basement (actually at street level). The yard opened in February 1903 and Bernard Road depot was kept open to deal with heavier loads. To avoid confusion, Bernard Road goods was renamed Nunnery Goods and the title of City Goods passed onto the new goods yard. The depot closed on 12 July 1965 when a new large freight transhipment and engine depot opened at Grimesthorpe.

Conisbrough railway station
The original Conisbrough station, near Doncaster, was situated some 150 yards (140 metres) to the east of the present one and had two sets of station buildings, one for the South Yorkshire Railway, its owners, and another for the Midland Railway, the operators of the first passenger service. Both had their own staff. This earlier station was opened on 10 November 1849, the only station on the new line linking Doncaster and Swinton. This was closed in 1884 with the opening of the new building, erected by the Manchester, Sheffield and Lincolnshire Railway. The buildings were in that company's double pavilion style and all except the former Stationmaster's house, on the Sheffield bound platform, have been demolished. Conisbrough station had three platforms with the Doncaster bound platform being an island. Nowadays it has two platforms and is served only by stopping services.

During Doncaster race meetings this island platform was used for 'ticket collection' to avoid congestion at Doncaster. In more recent times this platform was used for excursions which required an elongated stop for loading/unloading and could then enable another service to pass and use the other platform face. In April 1993, the station was equipped with ramps to give disabled access to the Doncaster-bound platform. Conisbrough station's most famous resident was film actor Donald Pleasance, whose father was stationmaster in the 1940s.

Conisbrough railway station staff.

Conisbrough railway station looking west.

Conisbrough railway station entrance.

Part demolition of Conisbrough railway station in 1986.

Conisbrough railway station, looking west, 2 January 2011.

Cudworth railway station

Cudworth railway station was opened on 1 July 1840 by the North Midland Railway. Originally called Barnsley, the station is referred to in R. Allen's Guide as 'Barnsley Station at Cudworth Bridge – Omnibus to Barnsley 2½ miles on the left'. On 1 August 1854 it was renamed Cudworth for Barnsley; In *c.* 1854 there was a new station; on 1 May 1870 it was renamed Cudworth. In 1885 the station was extended with an extra platform for the Hull and Barnsley Railway, which passed through but was not connected to the Midland system until the next century. In 1843, a luggage train collided with the rear of a stationary train in fog.

Then in 1905, once again in fog, two Midland Railway trains collided with a third. Post–grouping the station was operated by the London, Midland and Scottish Railway and closed to passengers in 1968. In 1988, the line from Wath Road Junction to Cudworth was closed due to mining subsidence.

Cudworth railway station.

This page: Cudworth railway station through the years.

Darfield railway station

Opened on 1 July 1840 by the North Midland Railway, the original Darfield railway station building was of typical Francis Thompson Italianate design. In 1901, the station was rebuilt (opening on 30 June of that year) forty-five chains further north next to the Doncaster Road. The new station had typical Midland Railway timber–panelled buildings. The new goods lines passed to the east. These had access to three major collieries – Grimethorpe, Dearne Valley and Houghton Main – and connected to the GCR and L&Y lines. Post-grouping the station belonged to the London, Midland and Scottish Railway. The station closed on 17 June 1963 and the line closed due to subsidence in 1988.

Darfield railway station.

Darnall railway station and staff: Mrs Kath Ledger and Mrs Lena Marsh. Darnall Station won an award for Best Kept Station on the Eastern Region, *c.* 1962.

Darnall railway station

The original station, named Darnal, which opened on 12 February 1849, was built by the Manchester, Sheffield and Lincolnshire Railway with two platforms flanking the main lines, the main station building was situated at the top of Station Road, and a waiting shelter gave passengers some comfort on the opposite side. In 1887 the station was renamed (Darnall) and during 1928 was rebuilt to an island platform design. Darnall was one of the first stations in the area to be de-staffed since tickets are now sold on board. The station is a shadow of its former self, with just a simple waiting shelter on its platform.

Darnall railway station.

Darton railway station, 16 June 1962. (Reproduced courtesy of *Sheffield Newspaper*)

Darton railway station

The Barnsley Branch (Crigglestone Junction to Barnsley Exchange) of the L&Y was started in March 1847, and all stations along the line, including Darton, were built in 1849. The line opened to passenger traffic 1 January 1850, with goods traffic begining to weeks later on the 15th. Train services are currently provided by Northern Rail.

Deepcar railway station

Situated on the line built by the Sheffield, Ashton-under-Lyne and Manchester Railway, Deepcar railway station, originally 'Deep Car', near Sheffield, opened on 14 July 1845. Located between Oughtibridge and Wortley, and built with two flanking platforms, the main station building was on the Manchester-bound side with a waiting shelter on the other. At the west end of the station, to the rear of the main line platform, there was a short bay from which passenger trains for Stocksbridge platform departed. This service, which commenced in 1877, ceased in 1931. Operations pre-grouping were conducted by the Sheffield, Ashton-under-Lyne and Manchester Railway and Great Central Railway; post-grouping by the London and North Eastern Railway and London Midland Region of British Railways. The station closed to passenger traffic on 15 June 1959.

Deepcar Great Central railway station, *c.* 1900.

Deepcar railway station.

Above is Deepcar railway station in 1986 (*John Law*). Below Deepcar railway station stands derelict, 16 January 1995. (Reproduced courtesy of *Sheffield Newspapers*).

Denaby and Conisbrough railway station

Denaby and Conisbrough railway station was a wooden structure and its facilities included a locomotive shed to house the branch tank locomotive. Built to serve Denaby Main and Conisbrough, near Doncaster, the station was situated just to the north of the Manchester, Sheffield and Lincolnshire Railway's (later Great Central) line between Mexborough to Doncaster. Access to the station was by a subway under the G.C. line. It was the southern terminus of the South Yorkshire Junction Railway branch from Wrangbrook Junction. This latter branch line, promoted by the Denaby and Cadeby Colliery Company, was operated by the Hull and Barnsley Railway and connected at Wrangbrook with its main line between Cudworth, near Barnsley and Hull. The next station northwards was Sprotborough (H&B) railway halt. Originally there was no connection with the M.S.& L. R. line, this was not put in place until Great Central days, opening on 13 July 1908 in order for that company to reach Brodsworth Colliery. The station closed on 2 February 1903, when passenger services were withdrawn.

Denaby halt or Denaby for Conisboro' and Mexboro

Denaby halt, or Denaby for Conisboro' and Mexboro to give its full title on the nameboard, was on the Dearne Valley Railway, and intended to serve the mining community of Denaby Main; though it was positioned some distance from that area, in what was described as 'a marshy wilderness'. The halt was located between Edlington halt, the eastern passenger terminus of the line, and Harlington halt. The DVR was operated by the Lancashire & Yorkshire Railway and was built in order to tap the coal traffic available in the area, which could be shipped through their port at Goole. The line offered a passenger service between Wakefield and Edlington, near Doncaster. The Denaby for Conisboro' and Mexboro halt was closed on 1 January 1949.

This page: Denaby halt with staff posing; Denaby halt with railmotor; Dinnington and Laughton railway station.

Dinnington and Laughton railway station.

Dinnington and Laughton railway station

Situated on the South Yorkshire Joint Railway line, the Dinnington and Laughton railway station was built between the villages of Dinnington and Laughton-en-le-Morthen, near Rotherham. Opening in December 1910, the station was served by a Doncaster–Shireoaks passenger service provided jointly by the Great Central Railway and the Great Northern Railway. However, the GNR left this arrangement after just one year and the GCR carried on, extending the service to Worksop in 1920. The service closed between April 1926 and April 1927 and finally in 1929.

Dodworth railway station.

Dodworth station

Dodworth station was built by South Yorkshire Railway and opened on 1 July 1854, adjacent to the level crossing which took the main Manchester road through the village. The station was rebuilt by the Manchester, Sheffield and Lincolnshire Railway in the last quarter of the nineteenth century in their double pavilion style. This station was closed on 29 June 1959. Part of the South Yorkshire Passenger Transport Executive's plan for the line was to reopen the stations at Silkstone (actually at Silkstone Common) and Dodworth. Dodworth was re-opened as a single–platform station, with car parking facilities from the commencement of the new timetable in May 1989.

Dodworth new railway station pictured on 15 May 1989. (Reproduced courtesy of *Sheffield Newspapers*)

Doncaster (Cherry Tree Lane) railway station

Doncaster (Cherry Tree Lane) railway station was situated in Hexthorpe Doncaster, and was the original terminus of the South Yorkshire Railway. Later to be known simply as 'Cherry tree', the station was first used for a special train on 29 October 1849, and it was scheduled to open for public use on 3 November of the same year. However, due to further work being carried out, the actual public opening took place on 10 November. The station was closed when running powers were agreed between the South Yorkshire Railway and the Great Northern Railway, which allowed the SYR to run their passenger trains into the GNR station in Doncaster.

Doncaster St James' Bridge railway station. (*Geoff Warnes*)

Demolition of Doncaster St James' Bridge railway station. (*Geoff Warnes*)

Doncaster's first railway station.

Doncaster (St James' Bridge) railway station

Doncaster (St James' Bridge) railway station was situated in the Hexthorpe area of Doncaster and was accessed from St James' Bridge, the main road link between Doncaster town centre and the railway community of Hexthorpe. The station was a little nearer to Doncaster than the South Yorkshire Railway's Doncaster (Cherry Tree Lane) railway station, being less than a mile south of the main station, adjacent to the Sheffield line. The station was built by the LNER to serve excursion traffic, principally bringing visitors to the town in connection with the St Leger horse racing festival held each September, although it was also used for seaside excursions leaving (or passing through) the town heading for the east coast, mainly to Cleethorpes. Access was by a substantial wooden ramp, stepped on one side, plain slope for cyclists on the other, from St James' Bridge. Platform facilities were minimal and consisted of a small office used by the staff, which came from the main station as needed. Never having a regular timetabled service, the station did not appear in timetables, only in 'Special Traffic Notices' when it was to be used. An official closure date has not been recorded but it was, however, in use until the late 1950s, maybe even later. There were three station platforms altogether, though whether the south bay was ever used for passengers is unkown. The station platforms were not removed on closure and were in situ until changes were made to the track layout in the area in the late 1990s.

Frontage of Doncaster railway station in GNR days.

Doncaster Railway Station

The station was built in 1849 replacing a temporary structure constructed a year earlier. It was rebuilt in its present form in 1938 and has had several slight modifications since that date. The station has eight platforms on two islands. Platforms 1, 3, 4 and 8 take through trains. Platforms 2 and 5 are south-facing bays, and 6 and 7 are north–facing bays. A First Class Lounge for passengers with 'First Open' tickets is available on platform 3A. The station has recently been refurbished and is directly connected to the new Frenchgate Centre extension in Doncaster town centre. The station now has a new booking office for tickets and information, three new lifts, refurbished staircases and a subway.

Doncaster railway station platform view.

Doncaster railway station Cattle Dock.

Doncaster railway station exterior *c.* 1910.

Doncaster railway station platform view.

Doncaster railway station new frontage.

Doncaster (York Road) railway station

Doncaster (York Road) railway station was built as a terminus for services on the Hull and Barnsley and Great Central Joint Railway in Doncaster. The line and its stations were ready for opening on 1 May 1916, but its five passenger stations at Snaith & Pollington, Sykehouse, Thorpe-in-Balne, Doncaster (York Road) and Warmsworth never saw a passenger train. The route duplicated that of other railways in the area and the stations were some way from the villages they were intending to serve. Doncaster (York Road) railway station was reached by a triangular junction from the main line just outside of town. The station itself was located just beyond the Doncaster Avoiding Line, in the fork of the old A1 and the A19 (York Road). The station was kept fully intact until the late 1960s when demolition finally came. The only passenger trains to work over the line were enthusiasts specials; the last of these was the Doncaster Decoy, which ran on 5 October 1968.

Doncaster York Road railway station.

Dore and Totley railway station.

Dore and Totley

The station opened as Dore and Totley station on 1 February 1872 on the Midland Main Line extension from Chesterfield to Sheffield, and was initially served by the local services on this line. The station site had previously been occupied by the Walk Mill – a water-powered mill in operation from the 1280s onwards used by the monks of Beauchief Abbey to cleanse and thicken cloth. The station was subsequently served by six or seven weekday trains and three on Sundays. In 1894 the station became the branch point for the new Dore and Chinley line (now the Hope Valley Line). The original northbound platform was converted to an island platform and a fourth platform was built to the west. The station was closed to main line traffic and became an unstaffed halt in 1969. Subsequently, the island and eastern platforms were demolished in the 1980s. Main line services from the south, therefore, can no longer stop at the station and the Hope Valley Line now runs single-track (singled in the mid-1980s) through the station, with trains in both directions stopping at the one remaining platform. The station was named Dore railway station from 1969 until 2008. The name 'Dore and Totley' was restored in April 2008 when the station received new Northern Rail-branded running in boards. Plans are being drawn up to extend the size of the station by 2014.

Dore and Totley railway station.

Dovecliffe railway station.

Dovecliffe railway station with signal box.

Dovecliffe railway station

Situated on the South Yorkshire Railway's Blackburn Valley line, Dovecliffe railway station was between High Royds and Wombwell Main Junction. The station opened with the line on 4 September 1854 and was originally named Smithley for Darley Main & Worsborough, but by the end of 1855 was changed to Darkcliffe and again in early 1860 to Dovecliffe. It was controlled by a signal box, which sat on the station roof. When the line opened, as a single line, there was no block working and when a box was needed it was required to be placed on the outer side of a bend to give better visibility. With the station buildings being very close to the level crossing, the only place where the box could be erected was on the station roof. Dovecliffe closed on 7 December 1953. Pre-grouping the station was operated by the South Yorkshire Railway, post–grouping the London and North Eastern Railway. The line through the station remained open until 1986 to allow freight access to Barrow colliery, although the through line to Sheffield was severed between Birdwell and Westwood in the late 1960s with the construction of the M1 motorway.

Dunford Bridge railway station.

Dunford Bridge railway station

Dunford Bridge railway station, on the Sheffield, Ashton-under-Lyne and Manchester Railway, opened on 14 July 1845. It was situated immediately east of the Woodhead Tunnel, within the Metropolitan Borough of Barnsley. The station consisted of two flanking platforms; the main, stone–built structure, with booking office and staff accommodation was on the Manchester-bound (Down) platform, while the Sheffield-bound platform (Up) had a large water tower alongside a stone–built waiting shelter. The area was controlled from a signal box positioned near the road bridge at the west end of the station, but this was replaced by a larger cabin, of the late M.S.& L.R. design, immediately east of the station buildings, on the Up platform. This station was replaced by a modern structure with the electrification of the line in the early 1950s. Still with flanking platforms, but now realigned with the line through the 'new' Woodhead Tunnel (opened in 1953), the main building was still on the Down platform with a simple waiting shelter on the up. The station was closed with the passenger services on the line on 5 January 1970. The Disused Stations website records:

> After withdrawal of the passenger service in 1970 the line remained in use until 17.7.1981, with the track between Deepcar and Hadfield remaining in place until 1986. Parts of the trackbed were then blocked by road construction preventing any future reopening. Much of the line now forms a cyclepath, the section to Dunford Bridge is part of the Trans Pennine Trail.

Edlington halt

Edlington halt's full title, as shown on the station name-board, was 'Edlington for Balby Doncaster' (with the words 'for' and 'Doncaster' in lettering half size compared to the others). It was a small railway station at the eastern terminus of the Dearne Valley Railway and built to serve the mining village of Edlington and the Doncaster suburbs of Warmsworth and Balby in South Yorkshire. Like others on the Dearne Valley, the station consisted of a bed of sleepers set at track level with an old L&Y coach body lit by a couple of gas lamps for a waiting shelter.

The large station sign was removed in the late 1920s and replaced by a simple 'Edlington' sign. Opening for passengers on 3 June 1912 the station closed on 10 September 1951. The passenger service was originally operated by a Hughes-designed 'railmotor', which was fitted with vacuum-operated retractable steps, thus saving on platform building.

Edlington halt.

The first passenger train from Edlington halt.

Earl Fitzwilliam's private railway station

The Earl's station was situated at the upper end of the Elsecar branch of the South Yorkshire Railway. It opened in 1870, and was used by the Earl's parties visiting the Doncaster St Leger race meeting. The trains used by the Earl were known and shown in railway publications as E.F.W. Specials. The station was of two storeys, the upper storey containing a waiting/drawing room where the Earl entertained his guests prior to departure. Works records of Elsecar show that these trains ran until 'the early years of the twentieth century'. The M.S.& L.R. issued a Royal Standard to the station to be flown when royalty was included in the party. The station was also host to other trains not connected to the St Leger race meeting for usage by Earl Fitzwilliam. These were the seaside excursions operated for the pleasure of the villagers, which were a regular feature before the First World War. Still standing, the station is included within the site of the Elsecar Heritage Centre. The first mile of the line, northwards from the Heritage Centre toward Cortonwood, has been re-laid after it was closed in 1983 with the closure of Elsecar Main Colliery and is now operated by the Elsecar Steam Railway.

Ecclesfield railway station.

Ecclesfield East railway station

Intending to serve the parish of Ecclesfield, near Sheffield, Ecclesfield East railway station was built by the South Yorkshire Railway on their 'Blackburn Valley' line between Sheffield Wicker and Barnsley. The original railway station was opened in November 1854 and closed just two years later to be replaced by a new structure, which had staggered platforms linked by a footbridge and buildings dated from 1876 and cost £1,985 (including sidings and approach road). The station closed on 7 December 1953.

Ecclesfield West railway station

Ecclesfield West railway station served the communities of Ecclesfield and Shiregreen and was situated on the Midland Railway, lying between Chapeltown and Brightside. Opening in 1893, the station was initially known as Ecclesfield, but was renamed to avoid confusion with the Ecclesfield East railway station. Ecclesfield West closed in 1967.

Ecclesfield West. (*Douglas Thompson*)

Elsecar railway station

Elsecar railway station, near Barnsley, opened on 1 July 1897 and is currently based on the Penistone Line and Hallam Line served by Northern Rail.

Elsecar railway station.

CHAPTER THREE

Finningley Railway Station to Kiveton Park Railway Station

Finningley railway station looking north.

Finningley railway station looking south.

RAF Finningley railway station, was used as a temporary measure in the 1980s. (*John Law*)

Finningley railway station and signal box, 3 January 2011.

Finningley railway station

The first railway station to be built at Finningley, near Doncaster, was some 500 yards (460 metres) to the west of the level crossing on the main Bawtry to Thorne road (A614). The second station, still in South Yorkshire, serving the villages of Baxton and Finningley is on the east of the level crossing, some 2 miles (3 km) west of the county boundary. It is located on the Doncaster to Lincoln Line. The Disused Station website states a Finningley Station opened on 15 July 1867, but it is unclear which one. Although the station closed to passengers on 11 September 1961, it was opened specially for trains from Doncaster to the Finningley Air Show in the early 1960s and on one occasion to serve the Royal Train when HM the Queen visited the air base. Today only the derelict platforms remain, along with the former station buildings, which are now a private residence, and the signal box, which remains in use to operate the adjacent level crossing. The Disused Station website informs: 'Following the closure of the ex-V bomber base in April 1995 the airfield was redeveloped as Robin Hood Airport, reopening on 28 April 2005 to serve Doncaster and Sheffield. Doncaster Council is now backing a proposal for a new Finningley station to serve the airport. In the long term the council are proposing to build a spur into the airport. The new station will be on the west side of the Auckley level crossing 1 mile west of the earlier station.'

Frickley railway station

Situated between Bolton-on-Dearne and Moorthorpe on the Swinton and Knottingley Joint railway, Frickley railway station served the village of Clayton. The station was situated about a mile north of the present day Thurnscoe and closed on 8 June 1953.

Goldthorpe railway station facing north, 2 January 2011.

Goldthorpe railway station

Goldthorpe railway station lies on the Wakefield Line 14.25 miles (23 km) north of Sheffield railway station. South Yorkshire Passenger Transport Executive, responding to increasing demand for Sheffield-Leeds passengers in the area and a lack of capacity on the Sheffield–Barnsley–Leeds line, sponsored an hourly service via Bolton, and opened brand new stations at Goldthorpe and Thurnscoe. Goldthorpe opened in 1988.

Goldthorpe and Thurnscoe halt

Goldthorpe and Thurnscoe halt was on the Dearne Valley Railway (DVR) between Harlington halt and Great Houghton halt, and opened on 3 June 1912. Pre-grouping the station was operated by the London and North Western Railway; post-grouping by the London, Midland and Scottish Railway. The station closed on 10 September 1951.

This page: Grange Lane railway station and staff; Grange Lane railway station and signal box; Grange Lane railway station.

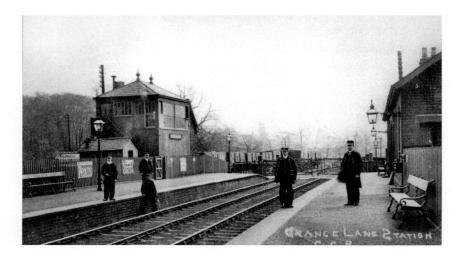

Grange Lane railway station

Grange Lane railway station on the South Yorkshire Railway line between Sheffield and Barnsley opened in June 1855. It consisted of two flanking platforms with buildings on each one. Both the line and crossing gates were controlled from a signal box situated at the end of the platform adjacent to the gates. Located alongside the lane from which it takes its name, the station became the interchange point with coal traffic from Grange Colliery (also known as Dropping Well Colliery), sunk in 1891. The station was closed on 7 December 1953 and most buildings still exist; the goods shed and both platforms survive while the station building is a private residence.

Great Houghton halt

Great Houghton halt was on the Dearne Valley Railway (DVR) and was originally named Houghton halt when it opened on 3 June 1912. It was renamed Great Houghton halt on 24 August 1912. Initially, trains were operated on behalf of the DVR by the Lancashire and Yorkshire Railway and later the London and North Western Railway took complete control. Closure of the station came on 10 September 1951.

Grimesthorpe Bridge railway station

This was a minor railway station and the first intermediate station to open – in 1838 – on the Sheffield and Rotherham Railway in Sheffield. Serving the communities of Grimesthorpe, the station was situated between Wicker and Brightside. The station disappeared from the timetables in January 1843; the old site is now underneath what is known as Grimesthorpe Junction and its complex trackplan.

Grimethorpe halt

Grimethorpe halt, on the Dearne Valley Railway (DVR) and situated between Great Houghton halt and Ryhill halt, opened on 3 June 1912, serving the village of Grimethorpe. The original operating company was the Dearne Valley Railway, pre-grouping London and North Western Railway, and post-grouping London, Midland and Scottish Railway. Closure of the station came on 10 September 1951.

Hampole railway station.

Harlington Halt.

Hampole railway station

Hampole railway station opened in January 1885 on the main line of the West Riding and Grimsby Railway and was situated between Carcroft and Adwick-le-Street and South Elmsall stations. It was close by and served the village of Hampole, near Doncaster.

The station's layout was a simple affair with wooden platforms and waiting shelters. There was a separate station master's house, which was situated at the roadside by the station approach. Hampole station closed on 7 January 1952.

Hatfield and Stainforth railway station, 3 January 2011.

Hazelhead railway station with staff and passengers.

Harlington halt

Harlington halt was on the Dearne Valley Railway near Harlington village, Mexborough. Services on the line began on 3 June 1912 and ran between Wakefield (Kirkgate) and Edlington via Ryhill, Grimethorpe, Great Houghton, Goldthorpe, Harlington and Denaby. From Harlington to Wakefield took 46 minutes. The station, situated between Denaby station and Goldthorpe and Thurnscoe halt, was closed on 10 September 1951. The Barnburgh and Harlington website states: 'The line did remain open for some time after that for freight traffic, serving the collieries along the route. As late as 1954, special day trips were run, twice a year, to the seaside.'

Hatfield and Stainforth railway station

This station was on the South Yorkshire Railway's line between Doncaster and Thorne. The original line closely followed the Stainforth and Keadby Canal and opened for goods traffic on 11 December 1855. The original passenger station opened with the coming of passenger services to the line on 7 July 1856 and closed on 1 October 1866, when the station was resited on the 'straightened' line. The new station opened on the realigned route away from the canal as Stainforth and Hatfield, but was renamed Hatfield and Stainforth in the 1990s; it was considered that Hatfield had the larger population

Hazelhead railway station

Hazelhead railway station, on the Sheffield, Ashton-under-Lyne and Manchester Railway's Woodhead Line, was opened on 5 December 1845, but closed in a cost–cutting measure on 1 November 1847. The second station was built on the same site in stone, with the main buildings on the Sheffield-bound (Up) platform and a waiting shelter on the other. A high signal box of the Manchester, Sheffield and Lincolnshire Railway's early type, almost square with hipped roof, controlled the station and the entry to the branch line which served the

Hepworth Iron Company's works at Crow Edge. An accident occurred at the station on 20 December 1907, when the lean-to building added to the station only a few years earlier was demolished. Hazelhead railway station closed to passenger traffic in March 1950 and to goods traffic in May 1964.

Heeley railway station

Heeley railway station, serving the communities of Heeley, Meersbrook and Lowfield, was situated on the Midland Main Line near London Road on Heeley Bridge, lying between Sheffield Midland station and Millhouses railway station.

Opening in 1870 at the same time as the main line from Chesterfield, the station had two platforms, but following the widening which took place between 1901 and 1903 this was increased to four. Heeley station was unusual as it was an elevated station with subway access from below to the platforms. It closed in June 1968, at the same time as Millhouses railway

Heeley railway station. (*Douglas Thompson*)

Heeley railway station. It is thought the picture was taken shortly before the line was officially opened.

station. The station building still exists and is used as a spare car parts shop, though no trace remains of the platforms. Unlike the Beauchief and Millhouses stations further south down the line, few pictures exist of Heeley station in operation because of its elevated position, the other two stations were alongside road bridges which the platforms could be photographed from, whereas Heeley station was the tallest structure in its surroundings.

Hellaby railway station

Hellaby railway station was an intended station on the H & B/GC/MR Joint line south of Braithwell Junction. It would have been served by trains from Doncaster, York Road. The station platforms were never built, but the goods station opened.

Hickleton and Thurnscoe halt

Hickleton and Thurnscoe halt was a small station on the Hull & Barnsley line between Wrangbrook Junction and Wath-upon-Dearne. The halt was built to serve the mining villages of Hickleton and Thurnscoe, near Barnsley, South Yorkshire, and was situated in the centre of Thurnscoe at the point where the line crosses over the main Barnsley road.

Hickleton village was situated over half a mile away. The station was situated 3 miles south of Moorhouse and South Elmsall and consisted of a single wooden platform with a single storey double pavilion style station building. The station opened on 28 August 1902 and closed, along with the others on the line, on 6 April 1929. The line was controlled by two standard H&B style signal boxes named 'Hickleton Station' and 'Hickleton Colliery'.

Immediately south of the station was the entrance to Hickleton Colliery where the H&B shared sidings with the Swinton and Knottingley Joint line.

High Royds railway station

Situated on the South Yorkshire Railway's Blackburn Valley line between Birdwell & Hoyland Common and Dovecliffe, High Royds railway station was one of the most short-lived stations in the county, opening on 4 September 1854 and closing just two years later.

Hickleton and Thurnscoe Halt.

Hexthorpe railway platform, scene at the time of the crash.

Hexthorpe railway platform

Hexthorpe railway platform was a short, wooden railway platform on the South Yorkshire Railway line about 1.5 miles (2.4 km) west of Doncaster in Hexthorpe Flatts, just on the Doncaster side of the road bridge. The platform was situated on the Doncaster-bound line and was normally used for the collection of tickets, particularly on the days of the St Leger race meeting. On 16 September 1887 the platform was the scene of a tragic railway accident. The death toll reached twenty-five and sixty-six were injured. The Hexthorpe rail accident was one of a series of accidents which occurred in the 'Battle of the Brakes', a period when railway managements were in dispute over the type of brake, if any, which should be used on passenger trains.

Holmes railway station.

Holmes railway station

Holmes railway station near Rotherham, serving the communities of Masbrough and Holmes, was situated on the former Sheffield and Rotherham Railway (S&R) line between Rotherham Westgate Station, and Wincobank and Meadowhall Station. Initially titled The Holmes, the station had two flanking platforms, and opened with the line on 1 November 1838.

It was renamed Holmes on 1 January 1858. Pre–grouping operations were conducted by the Midland Railway and post–grouping by the LMSR and London Midland Region of British Railways. The station was closed on 19 September 1955.

Joan Croft halt railway station

Joan Croft halt railway station near Thorpe in Balne, Doncaster, opened *c.* 1920 and was a small halt on the East Coast Main Line situated by the level crossing at Joan Croft Junction. The halt consisted of two flanking platforms to the south of the level crossing with brick –built station buildings on the York-bound side. These buildings still stand in private use. The station, set in the countryside with just a few cottages situated either side at some distance, was possibly never shown in railway timetables. It closed in the 1950s.

Kilnhurst Central railway station

Kilnhurst station opened in September 1871 (the 'Central' was added later) and the main building, which housed the booking office, parcels facilities, staff facilities and the station masters' house, was on the Sheffield-bound platform. It was built in the MS&LR double pavilion style, one of the earliest examples, while the Doncaster-bound platform had to suffice with a plain brick-built waiting shelter. Access to the station, for both passengers and goods, was originally from the Hooton Roberts road, but this was rarely used by passengers in latter years when steps to the road overbridge gave direct access to both platforms. The original operating company was the South Yorkshire Railway; pre-grouping Manchester, Sheffield and Lincolnshire Railway and Great Central Railway; post-grouping LNER and Eastern Region of British Railways. The Kilnhurst stationmaster also had control over another station, albeit both small and temporary. In 1959, at the request of the local Working Men's Clubs at Thrybergh, a short (about 75 feet (23 m) in length) platform was built near the Park Lane bridge on the Silverwood line to serve the 'Children's Outings' – seaside day trips for members and their children which were a regular feature in the club-land calendar. This was known as

Kilnhurst railway station, 28 August 1970. (Reproduced courtesy of *Sheffield Newspapers*)

Thrybergh Tins platform, but it never had a name board to that effect. The platform was used on three or four occasions each year and closed in the mid-1960s. Kilnhurst Central station closed on 5 February 1968. The last stationmaster was Mr George Adams, who moved to take over duties at Mexborough and amalgamated the positions at Kilnhurst with those of his new station until his retirement and the position of stationmaster ceasing. The Kilnhurst Central station yard was later used by Thomas Hill to rebuild /repair locos

Kilnhurst Midland railway station.

Kilnhurst West railway station exterior view. (Reproduced courtesy of *Sheffield Newspapers*)

Kilnhurst West railway station

Kilnhurst (later renamed West) railway station was opened by the North Midland Railway on 6 April 1841 and closed in 1851. It reopened in June 1869 and post-grouping was operated by the London, Midland and Scottish Railway. This station was served mainly by Sheffield Midland–Cudworth–Leeds stopping services. The station booking office was at road level, with an entrance on Highthorne Road, and was linked to its four platforms by a covered wooden footbridge. On 25 September 1950 it was renamed Kilnhurst West and closed on 1 January 1968. The line is still in use for freight, express passenger and local passenger trains.

Kirk Sandall railway station, looking west, 3 January 2011.

Kirk Sandall railway station

Kirk Sandall railway station was opened on 13 May 1991 by BR/SY PTE. It serves the suburb of Kirk Sandall in Doncaster, and is 4 miles (6 km) north of Doncaster on the Sheffield to Hull Line.

Kiveton Bridge railway station

Kiveton Bridge railway station was opened by the London and North Eastern Railway on 8 July 1929 to serve the growing communities of Kiveton Park and Wales and the now defunct Kiveton Park Colliery, which was situated adjacent. The station consisted of two flanking wooden platforms linked by an overbridge, access to which was gained through the booking office, set at road level adjacent to the main road through and linking the villages. In the 1950s the wooden platforms were replaced with concrete ones and the wooden station buildings by plain brick–built structures.

Along with neighbouring Kiveton Park station it was completely rebuilt during the early-1990s with modern platforms, lighting and waiting shelters; this work was funded by the South Yorkshire Passenger Transport Executive.

Kiveton Park railway station

The original Kiveton Park railway station was opened by the Sheffield and Lincolnshire Junction Railway in 1849, situated to the east of the level crossing and opened with the line. It was rebuilt in the Manchester, Sheffield and Lincolnshire Railway double pavilion style, on the west side of the level crossing in 1884. Kiveton Park was a centre of lime working in the area and many company sidings came under the jurisdiction of its stationmaster. The station was completely rebuilt during the early 1990s with modern platforms, lighting and waiting shelters; this work was funded by the South Yorkshire Passenger Transport Executive. The only remaining part of the 1884 station is the station master's house, which stands on the Sheffield-bound (Down) platform.

Kiveton Park railway station.

A modern view of Kiveton Park railway station.

CHAPTER FOUR

Maltby Station to Royston and Notton Railway Station

Maltby railway station.

Maltby railway station, showing an RCTS Special in 1952.

Maltby railway station

Maltby railway station was on the South Yorkshire Joint Railway adjacent to Maltby Main Colliery and opened in 1910. It was built in the double pavilion style by the Great Central Railway, who, jointly with the Great Northern Railway, operated a stopping passenger service linking Doncaster and Shireoaks. The G.N.R. left this arrangement after one year, leaving the G.C.R. as the sole operator. They extended the service to Worksop in 1920. The station closed between April 1926 to April 1927 and finally in 1929.

Maud's Bridge halt

Maud's Bridge halt was situated between Thorne and Medge Hall and was built by the South Yorkshire Railway on its line between Thorne and Keadby. The halt opened with the line in September 1859. Six years later it was at Maud's Bridge that the new 'straightened' track from Thorne South opened and the halt closed at the same time.

Meadowhall and Wincobank railway station.

Meadowhall and Wincobank railway station

Meadowhall and Wincobank railway station, also known at some time as Meadow Hall, was situated on the South Yorkshire Railway, lying between Grange Lane and Tinsley stations. Meadowhall station was opened in August 1868 and had two flanking platforms. The original operating company was the South Yorkshire Railway; pre-grouping the Great Central Railway; post-grouping LNER. The station closed to passengers on 7 December 1953. The line through Meadowhall closed completely from Friday 31 July 1987, and the line from Tinsley South Junction to Meadowhall was lifted during the following year. The main station building, alongside Blackburn Road, remains.

Meadowhall Interchange

Meadowhall Interchange, to the north of Sheffield, opened in 1990 and is on the Midland Main Line, a Sheffield Supertram stop, and bus station. It is close to junction 34 on the M1, and serves Meadowhall Shopping Centre. There is direct access to the shopping centre via a covered footbridge over the River Don. The railway station has four platforms: Platforms 3 and 4 for the Penistone and Hallam Lines, from Sheffield to Huddersfield and Leeds respectively via Barnsley, and platforms 1 and 2 for the lines towards Rotherham Central and Doncaster.

Mexborough railway station

Initially, Mexborough was served by two railway stations, Mexborough Junction and Mexborough (Ferry Boat) halt. Mexborough Junction station was opened by the South Yorkshire Railway at the point where the curve to Swinton on the North Midland Railway leaves their line to Barnsley, about 660 yards (600 metres) west of the present railway station. Mexborough Junction station was opened to passengers in January 1850 and closed, with the opening of the present station, on 4 March 1871. Mexborough (Ferry Boat) halt was a small railway station on the South Yorkshire Railway's line between Barnsley and Doncaster. It was intended to serve the township of Mexborough and the village parish of Old Denaby where it was situated, the boundary being the River Don. It is believed that the Mexborough (Ferry Boat) halt station also closed in 1871. The new Mexborough station was approximately halfway between Mexborough Junction and Mexborough (Ferry Boat) halt and was able to serve the town centre at the top of Station Road. Mexborough also once had a third platform which, in effect, made the Sheffield bound platform an 'island' platform. This was used occasionally for regular passenger services travelling via the Great Central line to Sheffield, but more often by excursion trains to the East Coast resorts, Scarborough, Bridlington and Cleethropes being the most popular. This platform face ceased to be used in the late 1970s but can still be seen. As part of the South Yorkshire Passenger Transport Executive's four-year plan for upgrading the railways in the county, Mexborough received an upgraded waiting area and ticket office, which were completed in May 1989.In 2009/10, Mexborough has undergone a further series of investments. These include help points, an updated PA system, refurbished toilets and booking office area, additional shelters, CCTV, information screens and improved access for the disabled.

Mexborough railway station looking east.

South Yorkshire Railway Stations

Mexborough railway station looking west.

Mexborough railway station staff; the lady is possibly Annie Grant.

Mexborough railway station looking west.

Millhouses and Ecclesall railway station.

Millhouses railway station

Millhouses railway station in the Millhouses' district of Sheffield was situated on the Midland Main Line between Heeley railway station and Beauchief station, and was accessed from the Archer Road overbridge, near the junction of Abbeydale Road and Millhouses Lane. When the station opened in 1870 it was called Ecclesall, but this was changed on 1 October 1871 to Ecclesall & Millhouses; 1 May 1884, Mill Houses and Ecclesall; 8 July 1932, Millhouses and Ecclesall. The station was opened at the same time as the main line from Chesterfield, with just two flanking platforms. Between 1901 and 1903 the line was widened and two lines added. The station now consisted of four platforms with two flanking platforms and an island platform in the centre. The station buildings were situated at road level with access by steps to the island platform. Operations pre-grouping were by the Midland Railway and post-grouping by the LMSR and the London Midland Region of British Railways. The station closed on 10 June 1968, and remained derelict for many years. The station buildings and platforms were finally removed in the 1980s, but the station master's house survives as a private home. There have been numerous plans to rebuild a station, going as far as a feasibility study in 1997, but so far none have come to fruition.

Millhouses and Ecclesall railway station and signal box.

Millhouses and Ecclesall railway station and staff.

Millhouses and Ecclesall railway station, July 1979.

Monk Bretton railway station

Monk Bretton railway station situated between Barnsley Court House and Cudworth was built by the Midland Railway in their characteristic country style with two flanking platforms; the main buildings being on the Barnsley platform. A signal box was situated at the outer end of the Cudworth platform; the station closed in 1937.

Monk Bretton railway station and staff.

Moorhouse and South Elmsall halt.

Moorhouse and South Elmsall halt

Moorhouse and South Elmsall halt was situated on the Hull and Barnsley Railway's branch line from Wrangbrook to Wath-upon-Dearne and located between Hickleton and Thurnscoe and Wrangbrook Junction, where the Wath branch joined the main line. Opening day was on 28 August 1902 and the single-storey station building, on the Wath-bound platform was, unlike the others on the line, built of brick with a slate roof. The other platform had just a simple waiting room for the few passengers who used the station. The platform surfaces were gravel and stone edged. The station master's house, of a standard Hull and Barnsley style, was situated at road level by the underbridge. The station closed on 6 April 1929.

Neepsend railway station.

Neepsend

Neepsend railway station, opened on 1 July 1888, was situated on the Manchester, Sheffield and Lincolnshire Railway's (latterly the Great Central Railway) Woodhead Line, which connected Sheffield Victoria and Manchester London Road. The station consisted of two flanking platforms joined by a footbridge, which also served to carry a footpath over the railway. The platforms were both served by small buildings in the pre-double pavilion style used by the M.S.& L.R. It was unusually located; the Sheffield-bound (up) platform was built against the face of a cutting while the opposite platform (Down) saw a long drop to street level. Operations Pre-grouping were by the Manchester, Sheffield and Lincolnshire Railway and Great Central Railway; post-grouping were by the London and North Eastern Railway and the London Midland Region of British Railways. Due to low public usage of the station, caused by the better-sited Corporation tramway services, it was closed to passengers on 28 October 1940, although the buildings and the signal box remained in situ until the 1970s. All traces of the original station have now been removed.

Neepsend railway station and train.

Norton railway station.

The Entrance to Norton railway station.

Norton railway station

A station was opened in Norton in 1855 on the Lancashire & Yorkshire Railway's Knottingley Branch. It was built on the Wakefield, Pontefract and Goole Railway line between Doncaster and Knottingley. The line and its stations were absorbed into the Lancashire and Yorkshire Railway in 1847, when that company changed its name from the Manchester and Leeds Railway. The station buildings were similar to those at Womersley and were described as 'Swiss Cottage' style. They are stone-built with a clipped gable end. At the grouping of 1923 Norton passed to the LMS and British Railways on nationalisation. The station closed to passengers in September 1948.

The remains of Norton railway station, January 2011.

Notton and Royston railway station

Notton and Royston railway station was a situated on the Barnsley Coal Railway between Staincross and Mapplewell and Ryhill. The station opened, along with two others on the line, on 1 September 1882, and had flanking platforms and simple buildings to house all the facilities constructed in wood. The station was closed to passengers by the LNER on 22 September 1930.

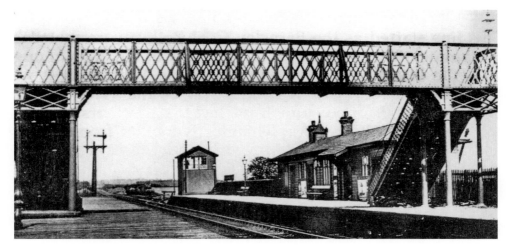

Notton and Royston railway station.

Orgreave Colliery platform

Orgreave Colliery platform, a workman's halt, was built to serve the miners at Orgreave Colliery. It was used by workmen's trains operated between Sheffield Victoria and Treeton Colliery at shift-change times. The trains were hauled along the main line to Orgreave Colliery Sidings where the main line locomotive was exchanged for one belonging to the colliery company. The platform was situated almost at the bottom of an incline with a steep gradient negotiated to reach the main line for the return trains. Often the train was reversed a short distance to more level track, enabling a good run at the gradient and a banking locomotive was also provided. The workmen's trains ceased running in May 1932 due to parts of the bridges between Orgreave and Treeton being washed away when the River Rother flooded. The line was repaired but the workman's trains were not re-introduced, being replaced by buses operated by Sheffield Corporation along the main routes from the city centre and the local area.

Oughty Bridge railway station

Oughty Bridge railway station was on the Sheffield, Ashton-under-Lyne and Manchester Railway, between Wadsley Bridge and Deepcar. It was opened on 14 July 1845 and had two platforms. Operations pre-grouping were by the Sheffield, Ashton-under-Lyne and Manchester Railway and Great Central Railway; post-grouping London and North Eastern Railway and London Midland Region of British Railways. Oughty Bridge railway station closed on 15 June 1959. The old station house, constructed from gritstone, is a grade-two listed building and has been used for industrial purposes for a number of years. In 2008 it was renovated and converted into a house.

This page: Oughty bridge railway station, 11 May 1985, (Reproduced courtesy of *Sheffield Newspapers*); Oughty Bridge railway station; Oughty Bridge railway station, pictured by Chris Lawton(of the *Yorkshire Post*), 8 October 2002.

Oxspring railway station

Oxspring railway station, built by the Sheffield, Ashton-Under-Lyne and Manchester Railway, opened on 5 December 1845, but due to cost–cutting measures it was closed, along with Dog Lane, Dukinfield, Hazelhead and Thurgoland, on 5 November 1847.

Parkgate and Aldwarke railway station

Parkgate and Aldwarke railway station was situated on the Manchester, Sheffield and Lincolnshire Railway company's line between Rotherham Road and Kilnhurst Central. Opening in July 1873, it was originally known as 'Aldwarke', and the principal reason for the station was its close proximity to two local collieries, Aldwarke Main and Roundwood. The stopping passenger service fitted in with the requirements of colliery workers and with many other workers living in Rotherham. Built in the M.S.& L.R. double pavilion style, with the main buildings on the Doncaster-bound platform and a waiting shelter on the other, the station also had the only wall drinking-fountain on the line. Other station facilities included a small goods yard with two sidings and a carriage and cattle dock. The station was closed to passengers on 29 October 1951.

Parkgate and Rawmarsh railway station

Parkgate and Rawmarsh railway station was situated on the former North Midland Railway between Kilnhurst West and Rotherham Masborough. On 1 May 1853 the station opened as Rawmarsh; 1 November 1869 it was renamed Rawmarsh and Park Gate; 1 December 1869 it was renamed Park Gate and Rawmarsh; 3 May 1894 it was renamed Parkgate and Rawmarsh. The original company was the Midland Railway; post-grouping London, Midland and Scottish Railway. The station and the adjoining steel works, together with other locations in the Rotherham area, were featured in the 1958 made film *Tread Softly, Stranger* starring Diana Dors. Diana Dors's co-star George Baker is seen arriving at platform 1 of 'Rawborough.' station. The station was closed on 4 January 1968.

Penistone railway station.

Penistone railway station looking east, *c.* 1910.

Penistone railway station

Penistone railway station is in the Metropolitan Borough of Barnsley. The current station (at the junction of the Woodhead Line and Penistone Line) opened in 1874, replacing a station solely on the Woodhead Line dating from the line's opening by the Sheffield, Ashton-Under-Lyne and Manchester Railway in 1845. This new station was by a joint GC & L & Y station with separate sets of platforms. Closure to passengers came on 5 January 1970 (GC Platforms only). After withdrawal of the passenger service the line remained in use until 17 July 1981, with the track between Deepcar and Hadfield remaining in place until 1986. The L & Y platforms at Penistone remain open, serving Sheffield, Barnsley and Huddersfield, with an hourly train in each direction. There is a voluntary organisation which supports and promotes community involvement along the line called the Penistone Line Partnership. The overgrown platforms and main station building are still extant.

Penistone railway station, 1980. (Reproduced courtesy of *Sheffield Newspapers*)

Penistone railway station, January 1977.

Penistone railway station, 2 March 1983. (Reproduced courtesy of *Sheffield Newspapers*)

Pickburn and Brodsworth railway station

Pickburn and Brodsworth railway station was opened on 1 December 1894 by the Hull Barnsley and West Riding Junction Railway and Dock Company. It was situated 100 yards south of Pickburn Lane, serving the villages of Pickburn and Brodsworth, Doncaster, and 4.5 miles (7.2 km) south of Wrangbrook Junction. The station was similar in design to that at Sprotborough closing to passengers on 1 February 1903 and completely on 30 September 1963.

Above: Penistone railway station, 16 May 1983.

Left: Pickburn and Brodsworth railway stationmaster.

Rossington railway station

Rossington railway station was on the Great Northern Railway's main line some 5.5 miles (9 km) south of Doncaster. The station opened on 4 September 1849 and was set slightly west of the old village. There were two platforms and post–grouping operations were conducted by the London and North Eastern Railway and Eastern Region of British Railways. The station closed to passengers on 6 October 1958 and on 27 May 1963 goods facilities were withdrawn.

This page: Pickburn railway station; Rossington railway station looking north; Rossington railway station and level crossing looking east.

Rossington railway station looking north.

Demolition and Rossington railway station, looking north.

Rotherham Central railway station

Rotherham Central railway station was originally named 'Rotherham', becoming 'Rotherham and Masborough' in January 1889 and finally 'Rotherham Central' on 25 September 1950. This was the fourth station to be built, within the town centre, on the line from Sheffield Victoria. It replaced a temporary Rotherham station, which was built with access from the road above named 'Amen Corner'. This temporary station served the town from 1 August 1868 and was short-lived, being removed as soon as the new permanent Rotherham station was opened on 4 March 1871.

This station was an elongated affair with staggered platforms and a large stone main building opposite the 'Statutes Fair Ground', with access from both Main Street, at the

Sheffield end, and College Road, at the Doncaster end. This station came under the ownership of the Great Central Railway when the M.S.& L.R. changed its name on completion of its extension to London (Marylebone station), in 1899. The station was served by Sheffield Victoria–Doncaster local trains and others ranging from the north-east to the south coast; the Great Central Railway was involved in many operations jointly with other companies. This station was closed on 5 September 1966 and soon demolished.

Stationmaster at Rotherham Central railway station, 20 September 1956.

The new Rotherham Central Station

The first sod of earth to be cut on the site of the new station was ceremonially cut by the Mayor of Rotherham, Councillor J. L. Skelton, on Tuesday 8 July 1986. The new Rotherham Central station was opened to passengers on 11 May 1987. The Doncaster-bound platform is on the site of the 1871 platform but the Sheffield-bound platform is now opposite. The station

Work on the new Rotherham Central railway station, 3 April 1986. (Reproduced courtesy of *Sheffield Newspapers*)

buildings, of modern brick construction, are at road level, with the entrance way through the ticket office; the platforms are approached by ramps. The P.T.E. funded the scheme with a contribution from Rotherham Metropolitan Borough Council to enhance platform shelter facilities. A grant for half the cost was obtained from the European Regional Development Fund. After just six months the passenger usage was recorded as being up by 120 per cent, compared with the old Masborough station for the same period of 1986. The official opening date was set for 2 June, however, this was postponed due to expected picketing by members of the National Union of Railwaymen demonstrating against the cutting of eleven jobs with the transfer of staff from Masborough and the concerns over the staff reduction on the platform at the new station, this being reduced to one person. Rotherham Masborough remained for the three per day Sheffield–York trains having regained its suffix, until its closure in 1988, when all services were concentrated on Central station. The station is being modernised and enlarged at the time of writing.

Rotherham Central railway station, 16 June 1988. (Reproduced courtesy of *Sheffield Newspapers*)

Masborough and Rotherham railway station.

Rotherham Masborough railway station

Rotherham Masborough railway station was opened as Masbrough by the North Midland Railway on 11 May 1840. The station, designed by Francis Thompson, had four platforms, with a large sandstone station building on the eastern Platform 4, large iron and glass platform canopies, a fully-enclosed footbridge and wooden waiting rooms on the other platforms. The station was renamed 'Masbrough & Rotherham' in 1896, 'Rotherham Masborough' in 1908 and it became simply 'Rotherham' in 1969. It closed on 3 October 1988, except for a few football specials. Most of the station buildings, awnings and footbridge were demolished in the early 1990s, but the platforms still remain, and the line through the station is still used by express and freight services.

Pete Ahmed, station supervisor, is depicted at Rotherham Masborough Station, 3 April 1985. The station won an award for Best Kept Station. (Reproduced courtesy of *Sheffield Newspapers*)

Rotherham Masborough railway station with Harold Hardy stationmaster. (Reproduced courtesy of *Sheffield Newspapers*)

Rotherham Masborough railway station, 30 September 1981.

Rotherham Masborough railway station, 4 January 2011.

Rotherham Road railway station

Rotherham Road railway station opened as Park Gate in September 1871, and was built in the Manchester, Sheffield & Lincolnshire Railway's double pavilion style with the main building on the Doncaster-bound platform; the approach was from Rotherham Road. The stationmaster controlled the small yard and interchange sidings on the Rotherham side of the station. This handled some of the traffic to and from South Yorkshire Coke and Chemicals works and, from 1873, via Earl Fitzwilliam's private railway, his colliery interests. The station, renamed Rotherham Road on 1 November 1895, was provided with a private waiting room reserved for the use of Earl Fitzwilliam and his parties when travelling to Doncaster for the St Leger race meetings. The station closed on 5 January 1955.

Rotherham Westgate railway station

Rotherham Westgate railway station, a single-platform terminus station, opening on 31 October 1838, was the eastern terminus of the 5-mile-long Sheffield and Rotherham Railway, the first passenger-carrying railway in the Sheffield/Rotherham area. The original station building was a substantial stone affair on Westgate itself, from where passengers had to cross the tracks on a level pedestrian crossing to access the platform. At the end of the nineteenth century this situation was remedied by giving the station access to Main Street and erected a temporary wooden station constrction there with direct access to the platform. The old station building became variously the GPO, a Labour Exchange and finally passed back into railway hands as a line–control office. The original operating company was the Sheffield and Rotherham Railway; pre-grouping Midland Railway; post-grouping LMSR, London Midland Region of British Railways. By the middle of the twentieth century, trains to Westgate still passed over the 1830s vintage-wooden bridge to call at the supposedly temporary wooden station buildings. It was the need to replace the decrepit bridge that prompted BR to close the station on 4 October 1952. The station lay derelict for nearly two decades, with the wooden buildings being used to store dismantled market stalls (the site of the town's market was opposite the station at the time) until 1970, when the site was cleared and a new Post Office sorting centre was built and remains to this day.

Rotherham Westgate railway station.

Royston and Notton railway station

Royston and Notton railway station was opened on 1841 by the North Midland Railway, but on 1 July 1900 it was replaced with a new station about a mile further south of the original site. The new station had four platforms and typical Midland Railway timber buildings, although only two platforms were used regularly for passenger services. The original operating company was the Midland Railway; post-grouping the London, Midland and Scottish Railway. The station closed in 1968. The GCR had a nearby station called Notton and Royston which closed in 1930. There is another Royston station built in 1850 on the Hitchin to Royston railway in Hertfordshire.

Royston and Notton railway station.

Royston railway station, 15 June 1962. (Reproduced courtesy of *Sheffield Newspapers*)

CHAPTER FIVE

Sheffield Midland Railway Station to Treeton Railway Station

Sheffield Midland railway station entrance.

Sheffield Midland railway station

Sheffield station, later Sheffield Midland, is in central Sheffield. Designed by the architect Charles Trubshaw and opened by the Midland Railway in 1870, it was the fifth and final station to be built in Sheffield City Centre. The station, along with Pond Street Goods Depot, opened without any celebrations and originally there were different entrances for passengers of different social classes. The original station buildings can still be seen on the island platforms 2 to 5.

In 1905, the station was given two extra platforms and a new frontage at a cost of £215,000. The enlargements consisted of creating an island platform out of the old platform 1 and building a new platform 1 as well as a new entrance. Offices were built at the north end of the 300-foot-long carriage-way rooftop. A large parcels office was built to the south of the main buildings. Two footbridges connected to the platforms – the one to the north for passengers, the one to the south for station staff and parcels employees. The tracks were covered by two train sheds or rooftops. One spanned platforms 5 and 6, the second platforms 1 and 2.

Wartime damage put the rooftops beyond economic repair, so they were removed in the autumn of 1956 and replaced by low-level awnings. In 1970, Sheffield's other main station, Sheffield Victoria, was closed and its remaining services from Penistone were diverted until 1981 via a cumbersome reversal to Sheffield Midland, which became plain Sheffield.

In 1972 the station was resignalled and its track layout remodelled. On 21 December 1991 the station was flooded by the River Sheaf, which flows under it.

In 2002, station owners Midland Mainline, instigated a major regeneration of the building. The stone façade of the station was sandblasted and its archways filled with unobstructed windows to improve views both from inside and out. Other changes included the improvement

Sheffield Midland railway station – exterior view.

Duchess of Hamilton locomotive at Sheffield Midland railway station 4 May 1985.

of platform surfaces and the addition of a pedestrian bridge connecting the station concourse with the Sheffield Supertram stop at the far side of the station. On 11 November 2007, East Midlands Trains, an amalgamation of Midland Mainline and part of Central Trains, took over the management of the station. In October 2010, East Midland Trains initiated £10 million worth of improvements. Renovated waiting rooms, improved toilet facilities, upgraded security systems and a new first class lounge on platform 5 are amongst the redevelopment work.

Sheffield Midland railway station and passengers.

Sheffield Midland railway station tracks flooded, pictured on 23 December 1991. (Reproduced courtesy of *Sheffield Newspapers*)

Sheffield Midland railway station and new information system, 30 January 1984. (Reproduced courtesy of *Sheffield Newspapers*)

Sheffield Victoria railway station from an old print.

Sheffield Victoria railway station

In 1847, the Sheffield, Ashton-under-Lyne and Manchester Railway merged with two other railway companies to form the Manchester, Sheffield and Lincolnshire Railway. The station at Bridgehouses (about 1 km to the west of the future Victoria station) had been outgrown and an extension and new station were planned. John Fowler was employed to engineer the extension and station. Fowler's design included a 40-foot-high, 750-yard viaduct over the Wicker and two island platforms 1,000 feet long. The extension was completed in 1847–8 and the new Victoria station opened on 15 September 1851.

The station gained a 400-feet-long, ridge-furrow-patterned glass roof which spanned the main line platforms in 1867 and was further enlarged in 1874; the well-known railway contractors Logan and Hemingway were awarded the contract. The station received a new frontage in 1908 and took on great importance when the line through the Pennines – known as the Woodhead Route which was electrified for freight purposes after the Second World War. The electrification of the line reached Sheffield Victoria by 1954, reducing the journey time to Manchester to fifty-six minutes. This was the first main line in the UK to be electrified, but the only one at 1,500 V d.c., a system which was already obsolescent.

Sheffield Victoria railway station exterior view.

Sheffield Victoria railway station exterior view *c.* 1982.

Sheffield Victoria railway station and evacuees.

Sheffield Victoria railway station and electric locos.

In 1965, the second Beeching Report recommended that the Sheffield to Manchester service be consolidated; after much local wrangling British Railways favoured the Hope Valley Line which was slower and not electrified, but served more local communities. Eventually, the enquiry backed British Rail's plans and passenger services were withdrawn from the line on 5 January 1970. The last train to Victoria station, an enthusiasts' special, arrived at 00:44

Sheffield Victoria railway station reopened for a day on 21 January 1973. (Reproduced courtesy of *Sheffield Newspapers*)

Sheffield Victoria railway station, scene as the last train leaves, 5 January 1970. (Reproduced courtesy of *Sheffield Newspapers*)

on 5 January and from that point the station was closed. The station re-opened very briefly in the early 1970s for diverted trains while Sheffield station was closed for re-signalling. Except for the goods avoiding line, which still exists to serve the steelworks at Stocksbridge, the track through the station was lifted in the mid-1980s and the station buildings were demolished in 1989 to make way for an extension to the adjacent Victoria Hotel complex.

This page: Sheffield Victoria railway station 1982; Sheffield Victoria railway station 1982; Silkstone Common railway station.

Silkstone Common railway station

The original station, simply known as 'Silkstone', was opened on 1 November 1855 and rebuilt on the same site in the last quarter of the nineteenth century in the double pavilion style of the Manchester, Sheffield and Lincolnshire Railway. The former station master's house remains towards the Penistone end of the present platform. This is now a private residence. The station closed in 1959 with the withdrawal of the Penistone–Barnsley–Doncaster stopping services, but was re-opened on 14 May 1983, after Sheffield–Huddersfield services had been diverted via the line.

Silkstone Common railway station.

Silverwood Colliery platform

The original Silverwood Colliery platform was a wooden railway platform built for John Brown's Private Railway in order to operate Paddy Mail trains from Roundwood Colliery to Silverwood Colliery to bring their workers to the new coal mine. These trains lasted until the 1930s, when either the workers at Silverwood had moved to new housing in Thrybergh, or were in a position to use the new 'pit buses' operated by private companies and later by Rotherham Corporation. The platform was removed shortly after the last train left.

The second Silverwood Colliery platform was a specially constructed railway platform built for HM the Queen, when she visited the colliery on 31 July 1975. The royal party stayed overnight on the Royal Train in Silverwood Colliery Sidings before the colliery visit the following day, when the platform was used for the only time, being removed shortly afterwards.

Spike Island

Spike Island was a workman's platform situated off the Great Northern Railway's main line south of Doncaster, and adjacent to the Doncaster Plant's wagon building and repair shops in an area known as the Carr. It was located off the Down Goods Line and was served by a passenger train, known as the *Spike Island Flyer*. This transported Plant Works staff from Doncaster station to work in the Wagon Shops and returned them in the evening. The service ceased when the Carr Wagon Shops, closed in the early 1960s, production being moved to the main Plant Works.

The name 'Spike Island' was given to the area around the wagon shops but its origins are unclear

Sprotborough railway stations

Sprotbrough's first railway station was half a mile to the south of the village on the other side of the River Don near the village of Warmsworth. This opened in 1850 and was located where the Warmsworth to Sprotborough road crosses the line over the deep-limestone cutting and was approached by a covered flight of sixty-six steps to the Sheffield-bound platform. The station had two flanking platforms and a small wooden shelter, which served as both ticket office and waiting room. Following the closure of the station on 1 January 1875, this structure served as a platelayers hut until the mid-1950s. It is sometimes referred to as Sprotborough (SYR). The second Sprotbrough Station, opened on 1 December 1894,

Sprotbrough's first railway station (in the cutting near Warmsworth) later became a platelayer's hut.

Sprotbrough railway station looking west.

was the line of the Hull Barnsley and West Riding Junction Railway and Dock Company. The main building, a single-storey wooden structure with brick-built chimneys, was situated on the Hull-bound platform, as was the signal cabin which contained a ten-lever frame. The Denaby-bound platform was provided with a wooden waiting shelter. A house for the stationmaster was built nearby and still stands. It closed to passengers on 1 February 1903 and closed completely on 10 August 1964.

Above: Sprotbrough railway station looking east.

Right: Sprotbrough railway stationmaster, Mr Howard.

Sprotbrough railway station with Hull & Barnsley Railway 0-6-2T locomotive no. 104.

Sprotbrough railway station.

Stairfoot railway station

Stairfoot railway station was on the South Yorkshire Railway's main line between Mexborough and Barnsley and situated between Wombwell Central and Barnsley. The original station, which was called Ardsley, opened on 1 July 1851, suffering a temporary closure between 1856 and April 1858 and was finally closed on 1 December 1871. It was being replaced by a new station built in the double pavilion style favoured by the Manchester, Sheffield and Lincolnshire Railway. The station was the scene of an accident on 12 December 1870, when a goods train divided, the rear section rolling backwards towards the platforms and colliding with a stationary passenger train, killing fifteen passengers and injuring fifty-nine others. Suffering heavily from bus competition, the station closed on 16 September 1957.

Stairfoot railway station.

Staincross and Mapplewell railway station

Staincross and Mapplewell railway station was one of three stations built on the Barnsley Coal Railway and opened when that line was completed on 1 September 1882. It was situated between Stairfoot and Notton and Royston and consisted of two flanking platforms with access from the road bridge. It is referred to as 'Staincross for Mapplewell' in the July 1922 issue of *Bradshaw's Railway Guide* and was closed on 22 September 1930.

Stainforth and Hatfield railway station.

Stainforth and Hatfield railway station

The station, known until the 1990s as 'Stainforth and Hatfield', was built in 1866 as a replacement for the South Yorkshire Railway's Stainforth railway station (which opened with the coming of passenger services to the line on 7 July 1856 and closed on 1 October 1866) when the station was re-sited on the 'straightened' line. The station was renamed Hatfield and Stainforth in the 1990s when it was considered that Hatfield was the larger of the two and had the larger population.

Stocksbridge platform

Stocksbridge platform was a small railway halt, the terminus of, and only railway station on the Stocksbridge Railway. It catered for the passenger service, which ran from a west-facing bay platform at Deepcar, on the Manchester, Sheffield and Lincolnshire Railway's Woodhead line. The service commenced operation on 14 April 1877 and ceased in 1931. Operation was undertaken by the Stocksbridge Railway Company, which bought two small coaches for the trains, utilising their own locomotive. Passengers mainly consisted of workers going to Samuel Fox and Company's works, and school children.

Summer Lane railway station

Summer Lane railway station on the Barnsley to Penistone line was opened by the Manchester, Sheffield and Lincolnshire Railway.

Swallownest railway station

This station never opened but was intended to serve the growing townships of Aston and Swallownest, east of Sheffield. It appeared in the British Railways Working Timetable very briefly in the autumn changes in 1993, being withdrawn from them at the following change (Spring 1994). The plan was to build a small station at the point where the Sheffield Victoria to Worksop line passed beneath the Swallownest to Beighton road on the south side of the villages. As part of the plan to increase rail usage in the area and with the expansion of Swallownest towards the line, this was considered the best location for a station which could then be incorporated into the timetable. Although the station appeared in the working timetable it never appeared in the public timetable or on other station timetables in the area. This showed all trains, in both directions, stopping. However, as the station was not built, it was withdrawn from the timetable at the following Spring changes.

Swinton Town railway station

Swinton Town railway station was the second railway station built on the North Midland Railway to serve Swinton, near Rotherham, and opened on 2 July 1899 when traffic was transferred from the first station. The second station was built to the north of the original one,

Swinton Midland railway station frontage.

and on the opposite side of the bridge that takes the road between Swinton and to Mexborough below the line. The main station building was at road level and comprised: booking office, parcels office and station master's room (this remains in existence at the time of writing). The station had four platform faces on two island platforms, one set between the Up and Down main lines, the other between the Up and Down slow lines. Access to the platforms was by a path and subway from the booking office. Both platforms had wooden waiting rooms. Train services ran to Sheffield Midland, Leeds City via Cudworth along the North Midland route, and Doncaster on the original South Yorkshire Railway route. In 1963 the station was refurbished and equipped with electric lighting, but along with other stations on the line the station closed in January 1968 and the platform buildings demolished shortly afterwards.

Swinton Midland railway station frontage, 2 January 2011.

Swinton Midland railway station.

Swinton Midland railway station.

Swinton, later Swinton Central railway station

Swinton, later Swinton Central railway station, situated on the South Yorkshire Railway line from Sheffield Victoria to Doncaster, was opened in April 1872, shortly after the through line, and comprised two flanking platforms. The main building, including booking office, porters' room etc., was on the Sheffield-bound platform and was a single-storey structure with hipped roof. The Doncaster-bound platform had, originally, a wooden waiting shelter that was replaced by a brick-built example in the 1890s. At the south (Kilnhurst) end of the platforms was an occupation crossing that gave access to the platforms as well. This crossing was unprotected by signals or any form of locking. The line was also crossed by a footbridge at this point with steps, not only to the thoroughfare but to the station platforms. The original operating company was the South Yorkshire Railway; pre-grouping Manchester, Sheffield and Lincolnshire Railway, Great Central Railway; post-grouping LNER, and Eastern Region of British Railways. Swinton Central was closed on 15 September 1958.

Swinton Station

In the late 1980s it was realised that Swinton/Wath-upon-Dearne/Kilnhurst lacked a station. So, the South Yorkshire Passenger Transport Authority put forward a four-year plan for the improvement of services and stations as part of their Rail Development Plan. This led to the re-instatement of the 'Swinton Curve', from the former North Midland Railway at Swinton to the former South Yorkshire Railway at Mexborough West Junction, the building of a new station at Swinton and the re-routing of all passenger trains via this route. Swinton station was opened in May 1990 by Councillor Jack Meridith, who unveiled a plaque at the opening ceremony. The new station has three platforms and a small bus station. This was to be the fourth station that had opened in Swinton and occupies land on which the first station existed. Immediately after opening, it was unstaffed, but increased passenger usage led to the establishment in the 1990s of first a small cabin staffed for the morning peak period only. The cabin was later replaced by a brick building for the ticket office, waiting room and toilet. It is also an interchange for local bus services to Wath and Manvers.

Swinton railway station, on 16 May 1990, Councillor Jack Meridith unveils a plaque.

Swinton railway station, 16 May 1990.

Sykehouse railway station

Sykehouse railway station was built on the Hull and Barnsley and Great Central Joint Railway between Thorpe-in-Balne and Snaith and Pollington. It was built with the line, which opened on 1 May 1916, but never opened to passengers. Despite that, it had facilities and the two flanking platforms were in situ until 1960. The station was controlled by a signal box situated by the level crossing at the end of the platform and this lasted until final closure of the line.

Sykehouse railway station.

A more recent photograph of Sykehouse railway station.

Thorne (Old) railway station

Thorne (Old) railway station was built by the South Yorkshire Railway to serve the town of Thorne. It was situated near the town centre on the first stage of the canal-side line to Keadby, which was opened in September 1859. The new line left the original South Yorkshire Railway just prior to arriving at Thorne Waterside, taking a right-handed junction towards the town centre. When the line opened this station was the terminus of the line. The canal-side line became redundant after new 'straightened' lines were opened in 1864, with new stations Thorne South and Thorne North, opening; Thorne 'Old' railway station closed in 1866.

Thorne North railway station

Thorne North railway station, opening in 1869 is one of two stations serving the north of the town of Thorne. The station is 10 miles (16 km) north-east of Doncaster on the Sheffield to Hull Line. Stopping services between Doncaster and Hull and beyond call at Thorne North.

Thorne North railway station looking east.

Thorne North railway station, 3 January 2011.

Thorne South railway station

Thorne South railway station, opening in 1866, is 9.75 miles (16 km) north of Doncaster on the Doncaster to Cleethorpes line. On Monday to Saturday daytimes, an hourly service from Sheffield and Doncaster to Scunthorpe calls at Thorne South. The station is on the old Manchester, Sheffield & Lincolnshire Railway, later Great Central Railway, line from Sheffield to Grimsby. The awnings once extended the full length of the platforms.

Thorne South railway station.

Thorne South railway station, 3 January 2011.

Thorne Waterside railway station

Thorne Waterside railway station, or 'Thorne Lock', was built by the South Yorkshire Railway as the terminus of its line from Doncaster. It was the first railway station to be opened in Thorne. The line was opened for goods traffic on 11 December 1855 and to passenger services on 7 July 1856. Passenger services lasted for around three years before being transferred to a new station, officially called 'Thorne' but usually referred to as Thorne (Old) railway station, near the town centre. A third station, Thorne South, on the 'straightened' line, replaced this from 1864.

Thorpe-in-Balne railway station

Thorpe-in-Balne railway station was on the Hull and Barnsley and Great Central Joint Railway, some 6 miles (10 km) north of Doncaster. It was built ready to accept passenger trains from 1 May 1916, but the line only opened for goods traffic, particularly coal, and that's how it remained until the early 1960s when everything was cleared.

Thrybergh Tins

In 1959, following a request by the local Working Men's Clubs at Thrybergh, a short platform was built near the Park Lane bridge on the G.C.& M.R. Joint Silverwood line to serve the Children's Outings – seaside day trips for members and their children which were a regular feature in the clubland calendar. The platform was known as 'Thrybergh Tins', but it never displayed that name on a board. The first train to use the platform ran on 17 June 1959, taking over 1,300 people from Silverwood Miners' Welfare Club to Bridlington. Thereafter the platform was used on three or four occasions each year. It did not appear in the railway timetables, the trains using the platform were shown in 'Special Traffic Notices'. The platform closed around 1968, although it remained in situ until early 1972.

Thurgoland railway station

Thurgoland railway station was built by the Sheffield, Ashton-Under-Lyne and Manchester Railway and opened on 5 December 1845. Due to cost-cutting measures involving staff and infrastructure the station was closed on 1 November 1847, making it one of the shortest lived stations anywhere, with a life span of just one year and 11 months.

Thurnscoe railway station

Thurnscoe railway station is located on the Wakefield Line 15 miles (24 km) north of Sheffield railway station. Only stopping services call at the station. It was opened as a new station in 1989.

Tickhill and Wadworth railway station

Tickhill and Wadworth railway station, originally simply known as Tickhill, operated its first passenger excursion, a Sunday School outing to Cleethorpes, on 6 July 1909. Regular services between Doncaster and Worksop, which stopped at Tickhill, opened on 1 December 1910. The station was built by F. J. Salmon of Cudworth in red brick with two platforms approximately 350 feet long connected by a footbridge, a booking hall, waiting room, porter's room, and goods' yard. The station was renamed Tickhill & Wadworth in 1911. The station was located on the South Yorkshire Joint Railway about half-way between the Tickhill and Wadworth on Doncaster Road at Gallow Hill, adjacent to the road overbridge which crossed the line.

This page: Tickhill railway station looking west; Scene at Tickhill railway station; Tickhill railway station.

The passenger service between Doncaster and Shireoaks was operated jointly by the Great Central Railway and the Great Northern Railway for the first year when the G.N.R. left the arrangement. The station was closed temporarily between April 1926 and April 1927 and finally on 8 July 1929, after a bacterial outbreak. Only the station masters' house and some remnants of the platform and the signal box's coal bunker still exist.

Tickhill railway station and staff.

Tickhill railway station and waiting passengers.

Tickhill railway station in 1982.

Tickhill railway station in 1982.

Tinsley railway station

Tinsley railway station was opened in March 1869 by the South Yorkshire Railway, on the line between Sheffield Victoria and Barnsley. It became a junction station with the opening of the line from Tinsley Junction (later Tinsley South Junction) to the original Rotherham station by the Manchester, Sheffield and Lincolnshire Railway. The station had two platforms, flanking the running lines, and was surrounded by sidings belonging to steel-works. The station was closed on 29 October 1951, though the buildings are still present near a new footbridge, which crosses over the line and Sheffield Supertram.

Tinsley railway station.

Tinsley railway station and staff.

Treeton railway station

The original Treeton railway station, situated on the North Midland Railway's line between Rotherham Masborough and Chesterfield in the Rother Valley near Rotherham, opened on 6 April 1841, but its life was short. A new station, on the same site, was opened on 1 October 1884. Pre-grouping operations were conducted by the Midland Railway and post-grouping the LMSR and London Midland Region of British Railway. The line here consisted of four tracks. The platforms served the centre two with access by steps from the adjacent road bridge; the goods lines was routed to the rear of the platforms. The station closed on 29 October 1951, although it was used for a small number of excursion trains after that date.

Tinsley railway station looking east.

Tinsley railway station looking east.

CHAPTER SIX

Wadsley Bridge Railway Station to Wortley Railway Station

Waleswood railway station. (*Douglas Thompson*)

Wadsley Bridge

Wadsley Bridge railway station opened on 14 July 1845 as part of the then Sheffield, Ashton-under-Lyne and Manchester Railway, on its original route from Bridgehouses in Sheffield to Manchester London Road – later more popularly known as the Woodhead Line. The station closed to regular passenger service on 15 June 1959, with the Woodhead Line itself closing to passengers in 1970. But Wadsley Bridge railway station still saw occasional passenger use – summer specials were advertised until 31 October 1965, Sheffield-Huddersfield passenger trains continued to run through the station until 1983 and football specials used the station until January 1994, serving Sheffield Wednesday's Hillsborough Stadium.

Wadsley Bridge railway station.

Waleswood railway station

Waleswood railway station was on the Great Central Railway's main line between Sheffield Victoria and Worksop. The station was opened on 1 July 1907 and was of all wood construction with flanking platforms. The station booking hall suffered a major fire on 24 May 1953, when much internal damage was caused and rail traffic was disrupted. The station was closed on 7 March 1955.

Waleswood railway station.

Warmsworth railway station

Warmsworth railway station was on the Hull and Barnsley and Great Central Joint Railway. It was built ready for the opening of the line on 1 May 1916 and although the line opened to goods traffic on that date, along with the other stations on the line, Warmsworth railway station never opened for passengers. Platforms were included and shown on signalling diagrams, but were never built. The only passenger trains to operate over the line were enthusiasts' specials, the last of these being the 'Doncaster Decoy' on 5 October 1968.

Wath North railway station.

Wath Central railway station.

Wath (Hull and Barnsley) railway station

Wath (Hull and Barnsley) railway station, one of three railway stations in Wath-upon-Dearne, opened for passengers on 28 August 1902 and was a single platform affair, but with a substantial station house. It was the southern terminus of The Hull & South Yorkshire Extension Railway, which became part of the Hull and Barnsley Railway in 1898 and was the southern terminus of a branch line from Wrangbrook Junction. However, the line was not a success for passenger traffic: it was closed to passengers on 6 April 1929. The station house and the former ticket office are the only surviving remains of the station and have outlived the buildings of Wath's other two, more successful stations.

Wath Central with No. 47222 in 1983. (*John Law*)

Wath Central railway station

Wath Central railway station was on the South Yorkshire Railway's Doncaster–Barnsley Exchange line and the closest of Wath-upon-Dearne's three railway stations to the town centre. The buildings were of the Manchester, Sheffield and Lincolnshire Railway's large double pavilion style; the main building, with four bays, was on the Doncaster-bound platform. The station was closed when local passenger services on the line were axed from 29 June 1959. However, the line was used for freight traffic until 1988 and the buildings were not demolished until the area was cleared during road improvement works in 2004.

Wath North railway station

Wath North railway station, on the Midland Railway's Sheffield–Cudworth–Normanton– Leeds main line, was opened as Wath by the North Midland Railway on 6 April 1841. On 1 May 1850 it was renamed Wath and Bolton; during April 1914 it was renamed Wath-on-Dearne; 25 September 1950 it was renamed Wath North. Post-grouping operations were carried out by the London, Midland and Scottish Railway and on 1 January 1968 the station closed when the local Sheffield–Cudworth–Leeds passenger trains were axed from the line. Express passenger and freight trains continued to pass through the station until 1986, when the line was closed due to severe subsidence; few remains of the station were present at that time.

Wentworth railway station

Opening in 1897, Wentworth railway station, on the Sheffield to Barnsley route of the Midland Railway, was known as Wentworth and Tankersley and Wentworth and Hoyland Common during its life. Built on an embankment, the platforms and the station building were high above the road with the station masters' house, which still stands at road level. The station's most regular passengers were Skiers Spring Colliery miners coming on and off their shifts. Pre-grouping operations were conducted by the Midland Railway and post-grouping by London, Midland and Scottish Railway. The station closed on 2 November 1959.

West Tinsley railway station

West Tinsley railway station, situated on the Sheffield District Railway between Brightside Junction and Tinsley Yard, opened on 30 September 1900 as 'Tinsley Road'. It had two wooden platforms each with wooden buildings. Pre-grouping operations were carried out by the Great Central Railway. The station also had a goods yard with a very large brick-built good's shed; these facilities were at the level of Sheffield Road and with access from that road adjacent to the road bridge. Under the control of staff at Tinsley West station were works sidings to Edgar Allen and Company and Firth Vickers and Company. The station was renamed West Tinsley on 1 July 1907 and closed on 11 September 1939.

West Tinsley railway station.

Westwood railway station.

Westwood railway station

Westwood railway station was situated on the South Yorkshire Railway's Blackburn Valley line between Chapeltown Central and Birdwell & Hoyland Common. The original Westwood station was opened on 4 September 1854 on a single line to the north of a level crossing. When the line was doubled in 1876 the station was staggered around the level crossing, reopening on 9 October of that year, with its main buildings, brick-built and similar to others on the line, on the Sheffield-bound platform. Although infrequently used by passengers, the station was a second point for dealing with the traffic generated by Newton, Chambers & Company. The original operating company was the South Yorkshire Railway and post-grouping by London and North Eastern Railway. The station was closed on 28 October 1940.

Wicker railway station

Wicker railway station (later Wicker Goods railway station) was the first railway station to be built in Sheffield, opening on 31 October 1838 as the southern terminus of the Sheffield and Rotherham Railway. Wicker station became obsolete as a passenger station on 1 February 1870, when it was renamed Wicker Goods and replaced by Sheffield railway station. The original operating company was the Sheffield and Rotherham Railway; pre-grouping Midland Railway; post-grouping the LMSR, London Midland Region of British Railways. Wicker station remained open as a goods station until 1965 and has now been demolished.

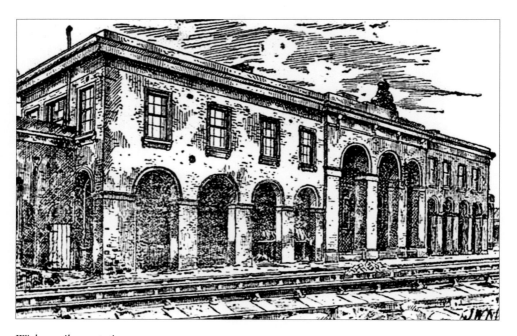

Wicker railway station.

Wincobank railway station

Wincobank railway station, previously named Wincobank and Meadow Hall, was in Sheffield, serving the communities of Brightside and Wincobank. It was situated on the Midland Main Line on Meadowhall Road, lying between Holmes and Brightside stations. The station was opened on 1 April 1868 and had two platforms, although four tracks went through. The two outside tracks were for freight use whilst the two inside tracks were used by both stopping and express trains. Only two were in general use as there were two slow and two fast lines. The station changed names several times. In 1868 the station opened as Wincobank.

Fire destroys Wicker Goods station on 31 July 1966.

It was renamed Wincobank and Meadow Hall station in July 1899 and back to Wincobank station in June 1951. The station closed in 1956 and the remains of the station were obliterated when the Meadowhall Interchange station was built on the site and opened in 1990.

Wombwell Central railway station

Wombwell Central railway station was situated on the South Yorkshire Railway company's line between Mexborough and Barnsley. The original Wombwell railway station was opened by the S.Y.R. in September 1851 and was replaced by a new structure in the Manchester, Sheffield and Lincolnshire Railway's double pavilion style in the 1880s. It was closed when the Doncaster to Barnsley local passenger service was withdrawn on 29 June 1959.

This page: Wincobank & Meadowhall railway station, *c.* 1947, looking towards Sheffield; another 1947 view of Wincobank & Meadowhall, looking towards Rotherham; Wombwell Central looking towards Mexborough.

Wombwell (West) railway station

Wombwell (West) railway station lies 12 miles (19 km) north of Sheffield on the Hallam and Penistone Lines. It was once known as Wombwell West to distinguish it from Wombwell's other railway station, Wombwell Central, which closed in 1959.

Wombwell (West) railway station.

Woodhouse railway station, 22 May 1980.

Woodhouse railway station

Woodhouse railway station, formerly Woodhouse Junction, is in Sheffield, on the Sheffield to Lincoln line. The original station, opened in September 1850, was situated at the bottom of Junction Lane, adjacent to the present Woodhouse Junction, formerly East Junction, signal box and was built to serve the communities of Beighton, then within Derbyshire, and Woodhouse. This station was closed on 11 October 1875 and replaced by one of the earliest examples of the Manchester, Sheffield and Lincolnshire Railway's double pavilion designs at its present location.

Woodhouse Mill railway station

Woodhouse Mill railway station was opened on 6 April 1841 by the North Midland Railway on its line between Rotherham Masborough and Chesterfield. Initially, it may have been a simple halt, but the Midland Railway installed an island platform with a timber and brick booking office at its centre. The station was located between Treeton and the original North Midland station at Beighton. The original operating company was the Midland Railway and post-grouping by the London, Midland and Scottish Railway. Woodhouse Mill closed on 21 September 1953.

Woodhouse Great Central railway station.

Woodhouse Mill railway station.

Wortley railway station

Wortley railway station, lying between Deepcar and Penistone, on the Sheffield, Ashton-under-Lyne and Manchester Railway, opened on 14 July 1845. The station was similar to the others which opened with the line, with flanking platforms, slightly askew and linked by a footbridge, and a main, stone-built structure with canopy, on the Sheffield-bound platform. Because of its proximity to Wortley Hall the station had a private waiting room for the use of the Earl of Wharncliffe, his family and visitors. The station closed on 2 May 1955.

Wortley railway station, 31 January 1955. Porter T. H. Lidgett hands a ticket to a customer.

Wortley railway station.

Wortley railway station, 31 January 1955.